*Changing Ourselves,
Changing the World*

Changing Ourselves, Changing the World

by

Gary Reiss, LCSW

Licensed Clinical Social Worker, Certified
Practitioner of Process-Oriented Psychology

NEW FALCON PUBLICATIONS
TEMPE, ARIZONA, U.S.A.

International Standard Book Number: 1-56184-143-9
Library of Congress Catalog Card Number: 99-61060

First Edition 2000

Cover by Studio 31

The paper used in this publication meets the minimum requirements of the American National Standard for Permanence of Paper for Printed Library Materials Z39.48-1984.

Address all inquiries to:
NEW FALCON PUBLICATIONS
PMB 277
1739 East Broadway Road #1
Tempe, AZ 85282 U.S.A.
(or)
320 East Charleston Blvd. • Suite 204
PMB 286
Las Vegas, NV 89104 U.S.A.
website: http://www.newfalcon.com
email: info@newfalcon.com

TABLE OF CONTENTS

Acknowledgements

I am thankful to my wife BJ and daughter Eliana for supporting me in my writing, especially in the midst of our many years of vacations together during when most of this was written. I also want to thank my parents and the rest of my family for all of their support, and especially for always encouraging me to write. I especially want to thank Dr. Arnold Mindell, who has greatly inspired me, and whose theories inform much of this book. He has been my teacher, friend, mentor, and role model as a therapist, teacher, and writer. Also thanks to Dr. Amy Mindell, particularly for her ideas around metaskills which are part of the background ideas that this book is built upon. Thanks also to Sharon Emery for her support and specifically for the many hours spent help putting this book together, and to Leslie Heizer for her excellent editing. I also want to thank the many Native American teachers who have been patient with me and helped me learn. All of these teachers have taught me the importance of personal growth and caring for the world, and how deeply connected these two threads are.

INTRODUCTION

I love small towns and could write many stories about my long-term love affair with them. However, this book is about much more than my love for small towns. I have been so nourished by the positive parts of small town living that I also want to contribute tools for working with the problems that lurk beneath the pleasant charm of small town life. In particular, I want to bring the tools of process-oriented psychology to small town problems. Developed by Dr. Arnold Mindell, process-oriented psychology is a unique approach to working with individuals, couples, families, groups, towns, and large world processes.

For the last twenty years I have been taking psychology into small towns, and small towns have helped me find ways to make psychology a tool available to all. Since its inception, Western psychology has often been used by highly educated, upper-middle-class people. This narrow application does not address the needs of most people. My own formal academic training reinforced the idea that insight—or awareness-oriented psychology—was only for the upper-middle class, while for others, pills or behavior modification were more appropriate. This is simply not true. People of all economic ranges, in cities and in small town environments, love learning about themselves, relationships, and families.

SMALL TOWNS AS MICROCOSMS OF THE WORLD

I will also apply what we can learn from studying small towns to the bigger world. I am disturbed by the world problems we face every day, and even more disturbed by the trend, particularly obvious in the United States, of people giving up their personal power to solve these problems. We give our power away to politicians who primarily serve the financial interests of themselves and a small part of the population. Over and over, I hear that people at the grassroots level have become apathetic because the world situation is just too overwhelming. I hope this book will help people study the world situation in a way that is not overwhelming; I also hope to show ways for people at the grassroots level to take back their power for personal growth and social change.

When we look at a small town, we see the world in miniature. In other words, the town is a microcosm of the world. The microcosm concept appears in a range of disciplines, including ancient religious traditions such as Taoism. It is also present in Western science. For example, I live on a farm that is state-certified as organic. We are required by law to provide soil for a laboratory test. To study our soil, we don't bring the whole garden. Instead, we dig up a cup of soil and assume that what the lab will find is representative of the whole garden. I apply the same concept in this book. It is much simpler to study a small town than a state or a country. Through watching the drug scene in our own small town, it became obvious to me that the federal government's war on drugs was doomed to fail. We will see more about this in the chapter on addictions.

One way to use microcosmic theory is to study a specific world problem in a manageable context. Another way to apply microcosmic theory is to assume that in every small town is the whole world. The emerging scene in the former Soviet Union is so complicated that even experts are having trouble comprehending it. However, it is possible to study a comparable scene in one's own small town. In any town or global scene certain roles will be played out. The names change, but the role remains the same. For example, there will be a reformer who is also a tragic hero, someone who takes the process of change far but eventually falls short of goals. There will also be voices of repression that will try to use their power to prevent change and radical elements that polarize against this force.

As we move through the chapters, we will first explore how small towns provide a forum to transform psychology into a grassroots tool. Then we will see how small towns serve as a microcosm of the global problems we need to address. These two points are related, since bringing the tools of process-oriented psychology to the general population might assist a shift in consciousness that would lead to people demanding political change. In addition, as people learn new ways to examine world problems, we may be able to reclaim our power to actively change our world.

STRUCTURE OF THE BOOK

First, we will learn basic information on process-oriented psychology, the theoretical base of my work and this book. Then we'll discover ways to be accepted in small towns, since those of us who want to bring the tools of psychology to more people need to learn how to be well received. Next, we will examine how small towns deal with violence, addictions, suicide, and relationship and marital problems, and discover the solutions small towns offer in these four problem areas. We will see how to deal with social problems at the small town level, specifically the problem of racism, and how to organize town meetings.

Part Two focuses on techniques that people can use by themselves and with their loved ones and families to expand their consciousness. A true grassroots approach to psychology supports people to grow outside the therapist's office, in keeping with the independent spirit of this country. We will examine several ways people can work on developing consciousness in their daily lives. Therapy can be an important addition to self-development, since all of us need help at times. But, just as in physical health care, we can learn to do more for our health at home and visit doctors when we need extra help. In a grassroots movement, the therapist supports growth and emerging wisdom, but is not the single source of growth.

Part Three looks at the small town as the world, and suggests new directions for involvement in and commitment to confronting the problems in our immediate environment and the greater world.

PART ONE

THE MANY FACES OF SMALL TOWN LIVING

CHAPTER I

THE MANY FACES OF SMALL TOWN LIVING

"Try imagining a place that's always safe and warm, come in, she said, I'll give you shelter from the storm."

—Bob Dylan

Over twenty years ago, I had had enough of city life. My bike had been stolen, my car broken into several times. Whenever I visited my parents, I had to avoid opening windows in order not to set off the burglar alarm. I became so hungry for nature that every weekend I drove to the country, where the air was clean, the views beautiful, and the store clerks friendly.

When I first left suburbia and moved to the country, I thought I had truly found shelter from the storm of modern civilization. For several years this illusion remained intact. Much of the safety, peace of mind, and natural beauty that comes with country living is genuine. People know and trust their neighbors. The urban burglar-alarm mentality is directly related to the amount of personal armor that we need to deal with the stimulating onslaught of modern life. In country life, this armor recedes and people tend to feel more alive.

However, because I work as a therapist, I quickly pierced this veil of perfect living. I have walked through the hidden side of small town life, where we find all the same problems that exist in large cities. Despite the fact that the same problems exist everywhere, I still look to small town and country living as a key to the difficulties of modern life. Not only are problems such as overcrowding and air pollution less dramatic, but problems are of a more manageable size. Economist and author Jack Lessinger predicts in *Penturbia* that we will gradually return to smaller towns for economic reasons. Other economists also predict resurgence in small town living, as urban life becomes increasingly intolerable.

I presently live in a town of about three thousand people, where the main attractions are a great video store and a horse auction. Sometimes I wonder how I settled here after growing up in suburbia. My ticket to small town living came on a vacation I took after breaking up with my high-school sweetheart. I had packed my bags and gone to the Ozark Mountains of Missouri for a rest. So many of my friends had married their high-school loves that I assumed I would also. When that relationship fell apart, my world shattered, which provided an opportunity to free myself from my known world and create a new life for myself.

I had taken Barry Stevens' *Don't Push the River* on my vacation. If I hadn't read that book, I might still be living in St. Louis. It was great medicine for my internal pressure on myself; I was pushing myself to be an honors student and to put my previous relationship back together. Stevens also talked about a Gestalt therapy training center founded by Fritz Perls in British Columbia. I was so taken that I wrote for more information, and it wasn't long before I was stuffing my car with suitcases and heading off to study.

Thus began my life work of studying different psychotherapy and holistic healing methods to help people with their problems. My journey to the Gestalt Institute also taught me about living more simply and being more independent, both psychologically and physically.

While I was living at the Gestalt Institute, I worked at a family social service agency in a small town. This was the beginning of my fascination with small towns and the sharp contrast between the hidden and revealed sides of small town life. While this dance between the hidden and revealed occurs everywhere we look, in small towns the hidden and revealed sides are clearly defined and observable. My experience with individuals, small towns, and societies as a whole is that they tend to identify with one side of themselves or another, but rarely with their whole selves. This lack of awareness of the whole creates certain difficulties, which we will explore together. The universal tendency to ignore certain parts of ourselves is useful in that it keeps us comfortable with our identity, but not so useful if we ignore parts of life which, without our attention, become problematic.

The hidden side of small town life is getting more attention in recent times. The United States was once a country of small towns, but as the number of people living in small towns has dropped, so has the level of public awareness about small town life. The problems of modern life appear even more dramatic against the background of a peaceful small town. How many times have you read about a mass murder or murder-suicide happening in a town you have never heard of before? A while back, I noticed news about two mass murders in small towns on the same page in the paper, then moved on to read about two murder-suicides in another small town in a different state.

In the late 1980s and early 1990s, two controversial movies exposed the unrevealed side of small town living. In "Blue Velvet," a college student visits the town where he grew up and accidentally stumbles on the actions of a dangerous, sadistic character. The young man gets caught up in this world and attempts to get people to do something about it. In "The River's Edge," a disturbed teenager lets out his frustrations by strangling his girlfriend. Both movies share a theme around individuals struggling to expose crime to create change, and both clearly show the common small town attitude of "Everything is fine in our town, so don't bring up problems." In both of these movies, there is the struggle to move past denial, a common response. It is hard to face the problems of life because they so radically disturb our image of the way things should be that we want to block out the difficulties. Denial is a huge problem for our country, and for many others. Denial can keep us from seeing and working with some of our toughest problems. We may be able to learn something about working with denial by exploring how some small towns have worked with denial and tough problems. Small town life includes not only mom and apple pie but also sexual abuse and amphetamine addiction, not only friendliness but tremendous violence.

I train therapists, and I always tell them that if they want to get a quick education about the wide variety of cases they may encounter, small town work is the best. Small town practice gives the therapist an exposure to the whole range of life, while many city practices bring therapists a homogenous group of clients. For example, a number of years ago a murder occurred in a small town near mine, and the mother was indicted for killing her six-year-old son. All of the people in the area were shocked. The Eugene *Register Guard*, our area newspaper, said that the image of the small town in which the mother grew up may never be the same. A local business owner was quoted as saying, "People in this area don't believe something like this could happen..." (*Register Guard*, Saturday, March 16, 1991, p. 4A)

Unfortunately, events such as this can and do happen all over the country, not only in cities, but also in small towns. Sometimes people are pushed by life to the point where they crack and do something that shocks everyone. This particular tragedy motivated our counseling service to expand its outreach even more. We want people to know how to get help when they need it, and to make help available to everyone regardless of income, intellectual level, or psychological sophistication.

The last thing our world needs is another book portraying how awful parts of our life are; when I read a book like that, I feel even more hopeless and despairing. This book is about how some small towns are facing reality and taking action. In the past three to four years in particular, I've seen real growth in terms of tackling some very difficult problems that threaten to shatter the myths of small town bliss. Therapists I know from other small towns around the country all report the same kind of problems and solutions we will see here. All of us can learn from how some small towns are taking on the challenge of facing reality. But before we bring frightening problems into the light where they can become more manageable, let's look at the positive sides of small town living.

The bright side of small town living is how fun and friendly the community can be. When I first moved to a small town, I got to know people in part because my car, a 1959 Volkswagen pickup truck, broke down so often that I had lots of opportunities to see how helpful people really were. Half of the people in town took turns pushing me to the gas station. Small towns have a slow-paced, humane feeling.

A strong spirit of community is healing for many people, and many of us long for it, especially as we experience the growing instability of the nuclear family. Intentional communities reflect the same need for community that small towns address. This search to belong to a small unit that is bigger than one's immediate family continues every day for many people.

Intentional communities and communes aren't the answer for most people in this country, yet the need for community is ever present. The model of the isolated family living without much support is no longer working, primarily because of the breakdown of both nuclear and extended families. As divorce rates increase, so does the percentage of single-parent families. Single parents are often in a terrible bind, forced to choose between an adequate salary and enough time with their children, which is the equivalent of asking if one wants an arm or a leg cut off. Even in small towns, the extended family is breaking up, although not at the rapid pace we see in bigger cities. People go away to college, leave to get jobs, marry and move away. This creates a longing for something to replace the extended family, and the hunger for a larger community grows. Small towns help address this need.

Beneath the genuine beauty of small town life, we find the same problems we face in cities and suburbs. When I worked at a social service agency in Canada, one of my first cases involved a family whose girl children were terribly bruised, supposedly from falling. I'll never forget one session I did there. I was talking to the mother and her two children, checking out the family for child abuse, while the father was remodeling the inside of the house, cutting something with a chain saw, glaring at me. The juxtaposition of the clean town streets with beautiful flowers at every house and this man and his abused children shocked me into the realization that, while the positive aspects of small town community life are true, there are also tough realities beyond the myths.

The United States developed from its small towns. Small towns and family farms were once its backbone. They played a tremendously important part in the political and economic development of the United States, but even more important, they carry much of the mythical element of our country and values. Just as the political and economic base of this country sprang from these towns, a new wave may emanate from them, a wave that could heal much of what ails us as a culture. It is possible that the next major shift in dealing with the problems that threaten our survival will not come from politics, but from a change in consciousness among all of us. If we can find solutions that work at the small town level, these methods can be applied with modifications to the culture as a whole. Just as the physical growth of this country began at the small town level, so may the wave of emotional and spiritual growth we badly need begin in small towns and move outward to the whole culture. People in small towns have some detachment from the overwhelming pace and input of the dominant culture, and this distance helps make small towns fertile ground for change.

CHAPTER II

AN INTRODUCTION TO PROCESS-ORIENTED PSYCHOLOGY

BASIC CONCEPTS

Until this point in modern history, we have lacked a single theoretical framework for thinking about individual psychology, politics, group psychology, and global issues. We have discovered important tools for helping individuals change, but how about communities or nations? What are our tools for changing the general level of consciousness on our planet?

Process-oriented psychology, founded by Dr. Arnold Mindell, provides a theoretical framework and tools for thinking about and working with individuals and groups of any size. Process-oriented psychology has helped me understand and work with my clients, my community, the world, and myself.

In this chapter we will briefly explore some of the main concepts of process-oriented psychology. In the following chapters, I will show how this approach has helped me learn to work successfully with small towns. We will then explore how some of these lessons can be applied to small towns in general, and to this country as a whole. By examining the microcosm of the small town, and the macrocosm of the United States, we will know more about where we are now and where we need to go as a nation and world.

One of the main concepts of process work is that life is a changing, evolving process. Process work is a depth psychology, which means that it works with both the dreaming background and the surface presenting level. The key question is: "What is nature trying to communicate to us in any given moment?" The process-oriented therapist uses specific skills to follow nature—for example, she pays close attention to verbal and nonverbal signals from the client, and discovers the best method of unfolding the message contained in signals by following the client's feedback. The process-oriented therapist is trained to carefully observe client feedback, and to have an open mind, testing interventions and drawing conclusions from the feedback. The process-oriented therapist begins with where the person or group is, and assumes that there is something meaningful about the state an individual or group is in. This kind of work takes a beginner's mind, that is, a mind that sees and experiences reality without being bound by preconceived notions. The concepts of believing in what is happening and watching for and following feedback are key elements of process work.

The basic concept of following nature and experience can be applied to a wide variety of situations both inside the therapist's office and out in the world. For example, a patient who has cancer comes into my office and says he wants therapy because he read that cancer is related to stress. As a therapist, I try to keep an open mind, study this person's life in detail, and stay open to the possibility that I may be able to help him with his cancer. Or a school official might come in and need help with growing racial tension at her high school, a project which I must also approach by seeing what is happening and helping it unfold into awareness. Even the most depressing life situations and cases become challenging and hopeful because, although the therapist and client may not cure cancer or solve racism, we will somehow facilitate growth in an individual or a town.

PRIMARY AND SECONDARY PROCESS AND THE EDGE

Another key concept that I will use repeatedly is that of primary and secondary processes. A primary process is that part of ourselves, or family, or town, that we identify with at any given moment. For example, now I identify myself as writing a book. This is my primary process. Many other parts of myself that I am not so aware of are also active. I'm writing at the ocean, on vacation, hearing the waves go in and out. But while I am writing I don't identify with the part of myself that is on vacation, only with the writer. If I want to do an experiment, I can stop writing for a minute and learn about this other side. When I listen to the waves I discover a part of myself that is concerned with bigger questions of life. The biggest concern I have now is where human existence is headed. My secondary process is concerned with the fate of humanity. Secondary processes are those parts of our lives that are more distant from consciousness and awareness. If I am going to write a book that comes from my whole self, I will need to include these greater concerns.

Individuals, groups, towns, and nations all have parts of themselves they easily identify with, and other parts that are more distant from conscious awareness. What separates these two processes is the edge, which is the point where we believe we have reached the limits of our capabilities. For example, let's say a woman comes to my office and says that she feels powerless with people, especially her husband. At one point in the session, she says she almost feels like yelling, but can't. This is the edge. Yelling is trying to happen, but the woman feels that it is beyond her abilities. If she can risk raising her voice, a whole different side of her may emerge, a side that might include her ability to be assertive.

As this woman becomes more comfortable with the part of herself that can yell, she may not need to yell much. Instead, she might become a clear and assertive person. In this case, the primary process, or identity of the woman, is a sense of powerlessness. The edge is to yell and get angry. When she yells, the woman experiences herself as powerful for a moment. Being powerful is her secondary process.

CHANNELS OF AWARENESS

While many psychotherapeutic approaches focus on one or two perceptual channels, process work is a multi-channeled approach. The basic channels of perception in process work include the visual channel, or inner and outer seeing; the hearing channel, or inner and outer listening; the proprioceptive channel, which feels body experiences and emotions, and the movement channel. In addition, there are composite channels made up of the basic perceptual channels. These composite channels are: the relationship channel, which includes the relationship between different parts of ourselves, or between two people or a family; the world channel, which focuses on larger groups and social issues; and the spiritual channel, which is the realm of altered states and spiritual experiences.

The most effective work, whether with individuals or with groups, happens when all of these channels are addressed. Most traditional psychotherapeutic approaches work in the auditory channel, and may include relationship as well. In traditional individual therapy, people may be taught to work with their thinking, to notice their self-talk, and possibly to work on their relationship communication. In more progressive methods, visualization may be brought in, but body experiences, movement, and social issues are rarely discussed and spiritual experiences are not explored. Process work helps facilitate growth by working with all of these levels.

LEVELS OF REALITY

Process work addresses three basic levels of reality. The first is the sentient level, which includes preverbal experiences and our deepest feelings and primal experiences. For example, the sentient level might be the experience of feeling anger as it first enters your body or your consciousness, experiencing it as pure energy before it takes on the color of anger or attaches to any thought, topic, or justification. Sentient awareness is connected to the first glimmering indications of experience that we feel;

usually we shut out our sentient observations, and they return to us in dreams, fantasies and physical symptoms. The second level is the dreaming level. In our example with anger, on the dreaming level, we would work with anger not only as something present in the moment, and something present at the sentient level, but also at the place where our night dreams and our body experiences reflect our anger back at us. I might think that I am in a great mood, but I have dreamt the night before of fighting with someone. Thus, anger is part of my experience. I might not think of myself as an angry person, but if someone presses deeply into the pain in my shoulder, I may suddenly experience a memory and fury may arise. Many times my clients will say they have no anger about a situation, while they pound unconsciously on the arm of their chair. The dreaming level brings in experiences that are present, but of which we were not previously aware.

The third level is outer, waking experience, ordinary consciousness, which is also the level where many psychotherapeutic approaches work exclusively. Let's look at how we might work with all three levels. A couple, Harry and Susan, come to therapy. Susan claims that Harry is a very angry man, and that she is not interested in or open to being angry. The couple has sexual difficulties, but also shares work and child raising in a fun and satisfactory way. The level of manifest anger is that Harry is always yelling. I address this with him, asking him if he can be more explicit in what he says and stick with his angry feelings rather than putting Susan down, which will cause backlash, especially in the realm of sexuality. I also ask Susan if there is a way she can let Harry know that she hears him, so he won't go on and on. This intervention works on the outer level of waking experience.

Next, I teach Harry and Susan some conflict work, so they learn to take each other's sides and not stay polarized. Susan says that she is not angry, but keeps having nightmares about violent figures. She also recently had a violent skin rash. In her dreams and in the way she describes her eczema, there is violence with which she doesn't identify. At this point, we are working on the dreaming level, and would go further by exploring the violence in Susan's dreams and skin rash. As we work further, Harry says that he is not aware of any part that wants to stop being angry once he gets started. I have Harry experiment with opening his mind and noticing the first body experience that grabs his attention. He notices the slightest feeling of his throat closing off a bit. As we work on this, a quiet yogi who closes off all outside awareness to go inside and meditate emerges. This is the deepest, sentient level of his experience. Contact with this side helps Harry learn to be more internal, which helps him break his chronic patterns of fighting and raging. We can see how working on the three levels of experience helps Susan and Harry develop in deep, sustainable ways in their relationship and within themselves.

We have seen that the edge is the border that separates parts from each other, the zone between primary and secondary processes. We tend to feel stuck at the edge, like we can't do or say or feel a certain way. In our example above, Susan came to an edge when I suggested that she follow her fist, which was banging on her chair, and be angry. Susan said that she could not do that because she would look like a fool. At edges, we find edge figures, specific internal and external voices that tell us not to change, not to go into new parts of life and ourselves. We also find cultural voices. In Susan's case, she heard her father's voice telling her to maintain control and not to embarrass him by becoming emotional. She also heard a cultural voice that said married women should not get angry because they could lose their husbands. Part of her work is to become aware of these edges and to make conscious decisions about them. Susan decided to try getting angry, which had the fairly immediate effect of bringing Harry into a more quiet, inward state.

SOCIAL ISSUES AND PROCESS WORK

In contrast to approaches that do not focus in the sociopolitical arena, process work often sees experiences in political and social contexts. Individual psychological and body experiences, relationship problems, and world conflicts all have collective elements and illustrate the struggles for change in the outer world. An angry man may be seen not only as out of control and needing to work on his temper, but as oppressed in many typical ways by being cut off from his feelings, overworked, and not appreciated for his whole self. Therapy may involve helping him face these cultural attitudes and doing something to change the world that perpetuates such attitudes. A person with a body symptom is seen not only as involved in a personal experience, but as carrying a piece of the collective world process trying to evolve through this person's body. For example, when I was working with a woman who had high blood pressure, we discovered that her blood pressure was fine when she asserted herself in her marriage, but when she gave up and became the subservient wife again, she put on weight and her blood pressure went up. She had personal growth and relationship work to do, but her body experience also reflected the changing nature of relationships between men and women.

APPLICATIONS OF PROCESS WORK

Process-oriented psychology can be applied to a wide variety of situations, including physical symptoms, movement, relationships, dreams, meditation and inner work, group processes, psychotic states and spiritual emergencies, comatose states, and organizational development.

The aspect of process work that includes working with small and large group conflicts and tensions is called worldwork. Worldwork focuses on addressing the problems of our times, including prejudice, war, environmental degradation, racism, sexism, ageism, homophobia, and classism. In small towns, therapists are often faced with situations that call for training in all of these areas. We will start by applying concepts of primary and secondary process and the edge to working with small towns. We will then study several different problems small towns face from a process perspective, focusing on drug and alcohol problems, violence, and suicide. Next we will look at how to work with social issues such as racism and homophobia using process work concepts and interventions. From here we will explore ways to work on oneself without a therapist in the context of small town living. The book concludes with a section on expanding the microcosm of small towns to the world at large. At this point, we will know some new ways to approach both personal and social issues, and will be able to challenge ourselves to make the world a more humane place.

PRIMARY AND SECONDARY PROCESSES IN SMALL TOWNS

Like people, towns have primary and secondary processes. As with individuals, there is often a strong identification with the primary process and strong resistance to identifying with the secondary material. For example, most small towns identify with being peaceful, folksy, friendly, and conservative. However, the therapist is privy to the hidden side of this town's life, which may be violent, full of addictions, and perhaps open to radical change. Secondary processes are not only negative. I often find that small town people are not at all conservative when it comes to their personal lives; they are often quite open to personal change. This openness to change is secondary in many small towns, and can be quite positive.

In order to help people achieve change and integration, it is important to be able to identify both the primary and secondary processes, and to know how to weave the two together. The change agent needs to know how to negotiate around the tricky curves that the structure of edges creates. It is the lack of weaving or connection between the two processes that causes difficulty. Most of us remain severely split off from much of the potential energy and liveliness that we have, because it lives in secondary processes with which we are not identified. For example, I have often worked with people diagnosed with chronic fatigue syndrome. For these people, the primary process, or identity, is of having little or no energy. On more than one occasion I have seen people who could barely get up off the floor access parts of themselves that were full of energy. While the primary identity is of having no energy, the "not me" part sometimes has apparently boundless energy. One person wrestled for half an hour, another did a wild dance. Secondary processes have different body experiences than the primary process does. Similarly, I have seen people with severe breathing problems, who usually have trouble with any exertion, get into a piece of work or be part of a group movement exercise where they make many movements with no symptoms.

Process work offers a safe access to the background energy that fills our dreams, body symptoms, emotional symptoms, and relationship issues. I once worked with a woman who had such severe panic attacks that she collapsed on the sidewalk, unable to move. When we accessed the power behind her panic, she had so much energy that she cleaned up all kinds of past issues in her life. The more she used her energy to clean up her life, the less panic she had. Her main identity at this time was as a woman on the verge of being dysfunctional; her secondary process was something like Superwoman, and she cleaned up her life at a faster pace than I had ever seen.

Let's look further at primary and secondary processes by examining some of the emotional patterns present in small towns. Although it is difficult to generalize, some basic patterns seem to characterize how people express feelings. The most common pattern I've seen is the combination of repression with an occasional big explosion. In the personality theory called Transactional Analysis, this approach is called stamp collecting because a person saves up feelings and then cashes them in all at once for a big explosion, an emotional breakdown, or an illness.

This pattern is quite common in relationships, and often occurs in the following form. One member of a couple calls and says they need an appointment immediately. Their relationship is in terrible crisis, and the trouble came up suddenly, when they thought everything was just fine. Suddenly one partner has bags packed and is ready to move out. If the therapist isn't careful to point out the need for follow-up, and to work with the underlying patterns, therapy usually continues briefly until the crisis calms down. Often there will be a second request for therapy when the next crisis occurs. The relationship style supports a primary process that everything is fine, and all the conflict in the background comes out only on rare occasions. Again, it is the lack of relationship between the primary and secondary sides that causes the extreme behavior.

This country as a whole has terrible problems with aggression, which we can see in crime statistics and our stockpiling of nuclear weapons. How to deal with violence and aggression is one of the most common problems I come across. In small towns there is a lot of support for being macho. In terms of aggression, this usually means physical fights. The problem becomes what to do with this aggression in relationships. If a person is working under the macho model, it is not acceptable to regularly express feelings in some way. It is macho to save up anger and then hit someone. This is a characteristic pattern of aggression, particularly in couples and families. There is no model for having healthy aggressive interchanges as a regular and nourishing part of everyday life. Instead, we save it up, ignore it, and wait for it to explode into domestic violence or child abuse.

In many cases there is also repression without explosions, and we may see bouts of depression and stress-related illnesses such as ulcers, colitis, and cancer. In these cases the repressed feelings are directed more at the person who feels them, rather than exploding outward at another person. This approach is supported by many religious approaches, by the small town values of kindness and respectability, and by military and work situations that emphasize conforming.

My counseling agency can predict the waves of clients with stress-related problems who appear after local factories lay off workers or cut wages. I have heard from local physicians and the local hospital that they see a similar pattern. Where do feelings go when one can't express them without serious consequences such as losing one's job? One answer is that the feelings block up our emotional systems. Optimally, emotional energy comes in, is digested, and what the organism doesn't need is eliminated. It's obvious what would happen to an individual who could eat and digest food but not eliminate it. A similar process happens emotionally, and we eventually become ill, physically and emotionally. We explode in part as an attempt to preserve our personal well-being, even though this last-ditch attempt creates a lot of difficulty. One of our tasks as a world is to help people express feelings in ways that are successful and workable in the particular context of their lives.

CONCLUSION

This chapter has introduced the basic philosophy of process work, which includes following nature, being feedback oriented, and finding meaning in life's experiences. We have seen how people and towns have primary and secondary processes and edges, and have touched upon the concepts of perceptual channels and levels of reality. We have seen that process work places an emphasis on social issues and have looked at a general application of the concepts of primary and secondary processes to small towns.

As we move into the next chapters, we will further apply the concepts of primary and secondary process and the edge to working with small towns as we study the problems of addiction, violence, and suicide from a process-work perspective.

CHAPTER III

CULTURAL PRIMARY PROCESSES

Let's look at how to work with the primary and secondary processes of a small town in a way that is useful to the town and also does not cause alienation between the town and the facilitator. Years ago, when I first asked local community members about starting a counseling center in my area, they said to forget it. Several private therapists had tried and failed. I was told that this town was too conservative for psychology, especially with a practitioner who looked like I did. A young, long-haired, bearded Gestalt therapist was the least likely candidate to make it in this town.

How did this situation change so that within five years we had ten therapists, a contract with the schools, and an excellent relationship with the hospital, churches, and other institutions in the community? It was partly luck and timing. Shortly after we opened, an agency director walked in and offered us a contract to provide counseling services. This really got us rolling. I was also able to apply what I had learned living and doing counseling in a small town before, and to use my training in process-oriented psychology to work with individuals, groups, institutions, and the town.

The lesson from my previous job was simple to learn but difficult to remember. I constantly have to remind myself that people are people and that if we are willing to open our minds and hearts we can find a place of common humanity in which to make a connection. This is step one in being an agent of change with a group of any size. It is easy to do with people who are like you and who you admire. Working with a client who is a murderer or child abuser or even holds radically different political or religious views is really difficult. Being open to people can't be a strategic intervention; it has to be genuine. When I moved to my town, I looked at what I really had in common with the people. Luckily, I love living in the country. I raise animals, garden, like to fish, and am a family person. This helped. I may have been completely appalled by my client's views or actions, which I would have to deal with eventually, but I could start with the fact that the person was an avid gardener. If an initial connection isn't made, I never get the opportunity to get to the material that needs to be worked on.

One of the cases that really tests my ability to connect is when I work with people from certain fundamentalist religions. They often want a therapist who not only shares their values, but their religion. Sometimes I need to refer people on to someone of their religion, but in a small town, there is often no therapist of their religion, and they have already gone to the religious leader of their church. Often I can connect with someone like this just by letting them know that I think religion and religious beliefs are very important to people, and that I study many religions. I often tell them about Jungian psychology, which is one of the pillars on which process work was built, and how Carl Jung wrote books on the importance of religion and religious symbolism to one's life.

Often simply valuing the primary process is enough for therapy to progress. You must first be able to join with what you are changing. This is the martial artist's way of bringing about change. As a child I studied judo, which means "gentle way." When you need to throw your opponent, you can use a lot of force and fight, or you just pick up the energy flow, the river's way. If a person is moving forward, you drop to your back, place your foot in their belly, and help them go forward. If they are stepping backwards, you help them keep going backwards by hooking their leg. It's easy. I was small as a child, and the class bully always picked on me. One day, after I had been studying judo for a while, he charged me. I dropped to my back, put my foot in his belly, and he flew. That was the end of the bullying. Whenever I can be in this river, I can help other people, and towns, to fly. The purpose of the psychological judo throw is to help people fly free of their old destructive patterns. Anyone who wants to be a change agent can do this; you just need to know yourself. Wherever you are naturally connected to a system or an individual, go with it. When the time for change comes, do the easy thing, and do it gently.

Sometimes it is right to push; sometimes violent, abrupt change is necessary, but often this just builds more resistance. Successful change agents address all the parts of the person. Process work helps with this by addressing the primary process, the secondary process, and the edge. Here is one example of how this applies to towns. The first time I went to approach a school for referrals, I blew it. I forgot to address the primary process, but instead went right into the secondary material. I arrived at the school and said, "I know you all are having a rough time, particularly with drugs and alcohol, and I would like to help." The person I was talking to said, "Well, we used to have problems. Everything is better now. We will call you if we need you." At this time, I had also brought with me a brochure that included classes in different areas ranging from speech therapy to Tarot and astrology. It was too far out—later these folks who became my friends told me that they were turned off by the Tarot class. I forgot to address the primary process of the school, which was that everything was fine. Instead, I went in and started talking about what was wrong.

Now, I would use a technique called talking to the primary process about the secondary. I would say, "I know things are going pretty well here. Since you are doing so well it might be hard to ask for help if you get in some tough situations, but I just want you to know I am around and available and really like working with tough situations. Give me a call if you need me." Speaking like this supports the idea that everything is fine in two ways. First, the fact that things are fine is acknowledged directly. Also, I pick up this theme indirectly in my style, by saying that even if there are hard problems, things are still fine, because I like working with difficulty. My general approach is very upbeat, which fits with the primary process of the town. This technique only works if you mean it, if you are genuine. People see through techniques that aren't backed by genuineness.

In this case I was lucky. I got a second chance when the school personnel came to me. At that time, the process had switched, and the primary process was, "We are really in trouble." I knew how to support that, and said, "How soon do you need me, I'm ready to go." The school representative responded with, "Things aren't that bad." I then said, "I understand, but it's wise to intervene and set up a program now before they get too bad." I got the contract, and we formed a mutually beneficial relationship that has lasted for years.

Edge figures are those actual or imagined figures that stand at the gate of new behavior and development and try to hold us back. Edge figures in a school are often saying, "If we admit our problems and aren't successful at improving them, the community may blame us, or stop voting for adequate budgets, so it's better to ignore problems." Typically, this edge figure contains limited wisdom. It is necessary to be careful with the community, but there are usually many more options than the edge figure presents.

For example, it does make more sense to deal with problems so that the community is really secure and the schools supported. Another point to consider is that those who are working in the schools will be blamed for school problems. It makes sense to act preventatively and to set up systems to deal with problems so that school personnel can say, "Yes, we are aware of this problem, look at what we have set up." Someone who wants to avoid disturbing people may want to say that they are working to prevent problems from occurring, rather than say that they are reacting to problems that exist. People are very open to prevention and less threatened by this concept. This particular school has done an excellent job of facing problems head-on. They found help for students who really needed counseling, and have since developed an excellent drug and alcohol intervention program. They have been able to keep some severely disturbed teens in school. The school also reflects a deep sensitivity both to the community and to the students, and does an excellent job balancing these two vital and sometimes different interests. In discussing specific areas of difficulty later, we will take a look at some of these programs in detail. Our agency has been part of helping create and maintain this openness by acting as a positive change agent for individual students and for the school itself.

The working relationship between our counseling office and the school has since spread to the medical community, and to state agencies such as family services. This small town medical community has been very open and supportive of counseling. In a small town doctors know who they can count on if they refer someone for counseling. As a counseling agency, we know we are in a small town, and if we don't do an excellent job, our reputation will suffer. One of the wonderful advantages to small town life is that people learn to rely on and trust each other. Building trusting relationships is crucial in helping towns and society transform. Trust is the bridge that spans the gap between the old and the change agents who can help bring about the new.

Let me summarize the steps that anyone who wants to be a change agent can take in order to form a strong working relationship with an individual or a group:

1. Identify and support the primary process.
2. Process the edge figures.
3. Access and work with the secondary process.
4. Integrate the new material with the primary process.
5. Be both relationship and result oriented. In other words, remember that you need to be both result oriented and

personable. Simply being friendly doesn't work—people need to see results. Simply being task oriented doesn't work—people need to feel related to and cared about.

Skipping these steps tends to create partial successes or failures. If the primary process isn't addressed, you are often not liked or trusted as a change agent. If the secondary process isn't accessed, you often don't reach the deeper levels of the problem, so that interventions either don't work or the situation looks fixed and then the fix doesn't last. If you skip the edge figure, it shows up later and causes trouble or sabotages the progress made. If integration is missed, the client can have huge breakthroughs, but then forgets them or doesn't really make the changes necessary to use the material gained from the breakthroughs.

Here is an example of how to address these steps when working with small town problems. The primary process of most small towns I have experienced is, "We are a friendly peaceful place, full of honest, hard-working, family-oriented, God-fearing people." Behind this primary identity is all kinds of secondary material, most of which is much less all-American. Sexual abuse is an incredible problem in most small towns, as are drug and alcohol abuse, racism, sexism, homophobia, violence, and sometimes, satanic cult involvement.

In most small towns, edge figures say things like, "Our problems are hopeless. Things are so bad that nothing can be done about them. If we admit we have problems, our whole world might fall apart. This is a small town, don't disturb the peace." These voices apply to the individual, the small town, and the world as a whole. In a way, the edge figure is wisely trying to blind us to many of our troubles—until recently there weren't enough positive solutions to deal with these kinds of problems. However, times are changing, tools are changing, and we must pull our collective heads out of the sand and do something about the problems we face. We must also be careful not to marginalize feelings of hopelessness and depression in communities. Until these feelings are addressed in small group gatherings, town meetings, and other public forums, they remain hidden forces that sabotage any positive suggestions made for community change. Once hopelessness, apathy, and depression are addressed, communities often regain their vitality and energy for making change happen.

Not only the culture at large but also the psychological and psychiatric communities have, until recently, feared unconscious processes in all of us. Treatment models have moved toward treating personal problems as medical conditions, rather than in the direction of relating to the person as a whole. When the unconscious rears its head in a condition such as a bipolar disorder, the standard treatment is to medicate this process back into submission. The basic principle is get rid of the process—medicate it, behaviorally modify it, hypnotize it away, psychoanalyze it away, but don't help this side live and move towards integration.

In *City Shadows*, Arnold Mindell writes extensively about psychologically effective interventions with people in extreme states. If this approach works with the most extreme cases, it certainly works safely and effectively with the everyday problems we experience in our lives. Thanks to approaches such as process-oriented psychology, our tools are changing. There are solutions, and the hopelessness need not be permanent. We now have road maps for how to deal with unconscious processes. Going hiking in an unknown forest is frightening and risky. Going into an unknown forest with clearly defined trails can be exciting and quite safe.

Let's say I want to address the situation of teen suicide, a nationwide epidemic that is highly problematic in small towns. Before I knew how to address this situation effectively, I attended a school meeting on the topic. The principal, with whom I had no relationship, told the audience that all the talk of recent suicide attempts was a rumor, that there were no problems, and that everyone should go home and forget about it. I got upset and confronted her, since I had recently seen four children from her school who had attempted suicide.

Later, I was given a chance to address the suicide issue at another school. I identified with the primary process and told the school administrators that I knew everything was going great at their school, but that I would like to talk about problems other schools were having, just as a preventative measure. Then I addressed the background hopelessness that came up.

Hopelessness is apparent in the comments that school officials make when they say they feel too overwhelmed to deal with the issue and that they cannot prevent suicide among teens no matter what they do. The edge figures are the voices that say it is better to ignore this problem, since we are powerless to change it. I addressed these edge figures by saying that I would help them with this problem, and that I had been successful in preventing suicide before. Together we could make a difference.

I then talked about the real dangers that existed, remarking on the number of young people from their school who had attempted suicide, and we talked about how to prevent such tragedies. Meanwhile, I kept up my relationships with the key faculty and administrators, making sure to bring them treats from my garden. I regularly visited to chat with the referral people. I made friends, talked to them about their families, about troubled children at the schools, about their own work loads. I let them know when I got results—when I had a release of information that allowed me to talk to them, I told them when my agency successfully prevented a suicide.

One day our agency got a call that showed us we had won their trust. Several teenagers were threatening to kill themselves together. We sent a team into the school and made sure that all the teenagers were fine. I then complimented the school administrators and helped them integrate this terrifying experience into their primary process, showing them how the school can keep its peaceful, positive image by taking care of serious problems, and by getting help that matches the seriousness of the problems. Classes went on as usual because the school was so proactive in addressing the issue. This example of covering all five steps can be adapted to many other situations.

CHAPTER IV

STEPPING INTO THE SECONDARY PROCESS — WORKING WITH VIOLENCE

A woman brings her loaded pistol into the clinic I run and asks us to keep it for her so she doesn't shoot herself or her husband. She says she can't take his lying and drinking any longer. A man walks into the local tavern and begins shooting into the air, upset over a relationship problem. A client calls me in the middle of the night, her voice trembling with fear. Her ex-husband is pounding on the door, brandishing a pistol. She has called the police, who told him to behave, but didn't take his gun away. I talk to the police and tell them to go back out there and protect this woman. Years before anyone thought about bringing metal detectors into city schools, I worked with teenagers who brought knives, clubs, and guns to their small town high school. Recently, in a school near my office, a young man opened fire with his semiautomatic weapon, leaving two dead and twenty-two wounded. In another school, two boys under the age of thirteen opened fire on students and teachers for no apparent reason.

This is obvious violence. Yet, when townspeople are interviewed about our small town, they always say they live here because it is so peaceful. They must not see the weapons brought into the office. They must not know how many women come in with broken bones and injured organs from domestic violence, or how many children have been beaten. In one of my first groups for teenagers, one young man talked about how he had gotten into a life of crime. He said it all started with his parents. They repeatedly had beaten and tortured him. Eventually the state intervened, and he lived in a series of foster homes. Based on these kinds of cases, I developed my ideas about working with violence, and integrated these experiences with my training in process-oriented psychology.[1]

With our process tool kit intact, let's explore violence, one of the most painful and difficult world problems. We will utilize a small town as our microcosm. We are a society preoccupied with violence, but we do not consciously identify with and process our violence. Many of us attempt to deal with our unexpressed violence through watching person after person murdered on television. Movie theaters draw crowds to films that show blood. Weekend football games offer vicarious relief for the week's frustrations. We attempt to hold off our violence with drugs like marijuana that keep us mellow, and at other times use alcohol, amphetamines, and other drugs that allow us to "let it rip." I refer to a frightening and frequent occurrence in small towns as "the nice quiet guy picks up a rifle and goes berserk syndrome." This happens in large cities as well, but it is particularly earthshaking in a small town, where everybody thinks they know everybody else well.

One headline in my local paper read, "Family Fights Bring Violence to Rural Towns."[2] The article says, "In small-town Oregon, victims of violent crime often have no farther to look than their own homes for their attackers. Despite the image of small communities as refuges from urban crime, six of the 10 Oregon towns with the highest 1994 violent crime rates have fewer than 8,700 residents, according to an Associated Press study. Nine of the top 10 have fewer than 20,000 residents." The article goes on to discuss the town of Phoenix, Oregon, which tops the list of violent places to live. "'If you were to ask any citizen in Phoenix if they were aware of the statistic, or if

---

[1] For those interested in further exploring this topic, see my *Angry Men, Angry World—A Process-Oriented Approach To Working With Anger*, forthcoming in 2000.

[2] The Eugene Oregon, *Register Guard*, Saturday, July 6, 1996, p. 3A.

the numbers seemed extraordinarily high, they would be amazed,' said Mayor Jerry Greer." Half of the violent crime reported was domestic violence, an issue that I address further in the chapters on aggression.

Several cases come to mind. In one small town the mass murderer was described as quiet and friendly—a member of the old-car club. There is the case of a postal employee in a small town who lost his job and then came back and opened fire on the office, killing a number of people. The universal response in cases like this is, "We never thought something like that would happen here. Nothing much out of the ordinary ever happens here. This is a nice quiet place." Out of this quiet scene the monster rears its head. The culture as a whole reacts by building more prisons and implementing tougher sentences, while treatment and prevention efforts fall by the wayside.

Those of us interested in prevention as well as treatment must often work without the benefit of government funding or programs. Treatment of the individual is not sufficient; we need to understand and work with violence in our culture. Otherwise, person after person plays out the role of the one possessed by violence. As a culture we are possessed; therefore we must make a tremendous effort to make this violence conscious enough to work with. We need to find and address the root causes of violence. We must address domestic violence and the sexism behind it, and the oppression of poverty and the violence that emerges from this oppression. We must also face the enormous amount of child abuse that continues to go untreated, creating multi-generational patterns of abuse, with the potential for each hurt to propel us into further abuse and violence.

Bringing violence into consciousness must be done on the individual, town, and world levels. In Part Three, we will discuss ways to work with anger in individual therapy. It is also vital to have school meetings and town meetings in which violence can be processed. One way to do this is by identifying the violent one as a role, not just an individual. Someone can play the role of the violent student or community member, while other participants can listen and interact with the violence as a role, thus giving it a chance to transform before it erupts for real. One way to go further with processing violence would be in regular school assemblies where students could work on what is really bothering them. This provides a forum for violence to be worked with consciously.

I regularly work in Israel, amidst growing tension between Orthodox and Reform Jews, conservative and secular Jews, and right- and left-wing Jews. I led one workshop in Jerusalem where the various sides had an opportunity to interact with each other. This was just after there had been several violent confrontations at the holiest Jewish sight, the Wailing Wall of the Old Temple. In a powerful confrontation the first night, we processed the violence in the air. The most charged encounter was between a woman who identified herself as a settler and an Orthodox Jew, and a woman who identified herself as a left-wing secular Jew involved in Palestinian rights. The hostility was so direct, and the group gave so much support to both sides, that something besides violence happened. By the end of the first night, the women talked to each other about how they respected each other's strength, while hating the views they stood for. By the end of the second day, the settler played a peace song that Prime Minister Rabin had sung right before he was assassinated. The secular Jew, who said she had been so depressed by recent events that she had given up singing, sang. This touching moment of healing would have made Rabin proud. Out of the potential violence came momentary healing, respect, music, and tears.

In the clinic where I work, we see the whole violence continuum—from teenagers who have committed violent crimes, to teenagers whose repression of their anger finds expression in the teen's depression, psychosomatic systoms like ulcers, and in other ways. The depression or ulcer might be pointing out the need for more expression.

I see teenagers who have pulled weapons on their parents, and those who need years of therapy before they are able to express anger. I've seen couples who have been thrown out of several therapists' offices because they are so violent, and once saw a woman who didn't come for counseling until her husband shot at her. Before this she didn't think they had a problem. Being conscious about aggression takes a great deal of work in a culture that has so little awareness in this area.

For example, I saw a couple where the man was beginning to be violent with the woman. She viewed herself as helpless and unable to stand up to him. After a number of sessions where we worked on the man's learning to change and express his aggression verbally and in non-damaging ways, the woman said she just couldn't stand up to him in any way possible, even verbally. At this point the man had stopped his physical threats. I asked the woman if she would do some movement work, as we seemed stuck in the couple's work. She said yes, and I asked her to push on my hands. She pushed with so much force that she threw me across the room and over a chair. She was stunned at the power inside her. In the next sessions, she learned to be in touch with that power and to use it to stand up to her husband in their verbal fights. The relationship transformed, and the woman began to be more in charge of her own life and her relationship.

I remember another couple in which the man had a long history of being violent with his partners. At a time when I saw this couple, he was being increasingly violent with his partner. In the middle of the session, I told him he had to stop the abuse. I supported his partner in ending the relationship if he didn't. I told him that he had to use his power to be verbal and say what he was feeling. He was so stunned that he sat down. He said, "You can't do that in a relationship with a woman." We had a long talk. He began to cry and said that he hadn't known a man could be this way. Every man he knew beat his wife, and he couldn't imagine a woman being with him if he expressed his feelings. He cried for all the pain he had gone through for so many years, never understanding why woman after woman dropped him. His partner said that if he were more emotionally and verbally expressive, she would love him more and not leave him. This was a new beginning, although more work still needed to be done after he made a change from violent to consciously angry.

This example captures a key process-oriented view about working with violence. Violence can't be ignored in therapy; it must be explored and transformed. One of the most dangerous cases I ever worked on involved a teenager and his mother. The teenager was totally out of control at home and had threatened his mother with weapons. In the office we explored what was behind the violence and, at one point, he backed his mother into a corner. I myself was scared and said so. I asked him to remember that this was his mother and, as angry as he was, he had also told me how much he loved her and didn't want to hurt her. Several weeks later they came in and told the following story. At one point a fight had gotten so severe that the teenager again pulled a shotgun on his mother and was going to pull the trigger. Then he remembered the work we had done and remembered to think about how much he loved and needed her. This was the last time he ever pulled a weapon on her, and they started to work in therapy and resolve the background issues.

This happened when I was a fairly new therapist, and I have studied this case many times over the years. Both mom and son said that the work we had done had somehow given him the extra edge of awareness to face his violence and not carry it through. This central issue of lack of awareness around violence must be addressed. Violent states block out other parts of oneself. Process work trains people to be prepared if strong or violent feelings arise, to stay aware of other parts of themselves. I have worked with several men who smashed their fists into walls when they got angry, thus breaking their bones. I had to teach them to listen to their rage and equally to listen to their hands that didn't want to be broken. This kind of awareness training is important and necessary. Many therapists, by avoiding facing violence, actually increase the possibility of violence happening. People need to be trained to be modern-day warriors who don't deny their feelings, but who don't just act them out.

In *King, Warrior, Magician, Lover*, Robert Moore and Douglas Gillette talk about warrior energy. "The Warrior energy is concerned with skill, power, and accuracy, and with control, both inner and outer, psychological and physical."[3] They go on to say that a warrior is appropriate with aggression. "How does the man accessing the Warrior know what aggressiveness is appropriate under the circumstances? He knows through clarity of thinking, through discernment. The warrior is always alert. He is always awake.... He knows how to focus his mind and his body. He is what the samurai called 'mindful.'"[4] Moore and Gillette suggest that people can learn to be aware in the strong altered states that aggression brings up.

THE MODERN WARRIOR

The trick now is to apply this teaching in everyday life. Let's examine in detail the issue of violence and what can be done about it. Aggressive behavior is a survival tactic. The ability to respond under attack is nature's way of protection. In less modern times humans needed their fight response more often—when a saber-toothed tiger came charging at you, you needed to know how to throw your spear in order not to be killed. There was a direct link between what got your adrenaline going and what you released your aggression against. In contrast, let's take a modern example—you are in a terrible traffic jam. Rather than a tiger, you fear your boss who is going to take your head off when you arrive at work. You express your rage by driving fast, maybe honking your horn or swearing at anoth-

---

[3] Robert Moore and Douglas Gillette, *King, Warrior, Magician, Lover*, p. 83

[4] Op. cit.

er driver. When you arrive at work, the boss calls you an idiot. You are so angry you want to punch him, but you quietly go off to work. After a rough day and traffic jam on the way home you are almost homicidal. Now, what to do with the anger? Repress it and get a stomachache? Take it out on your wife or husband, children, or dog? Watch several police dramas on television, hoping that after enough people get shot you will feel better?

Extreme examples of misdirected rage occur when someone opens fire on the freeway or walks into a tavern and begins shooting into the air. Many people are so hurt and angry that they don't care where, or towards whom, they direct their anger. It takes a modern-day warrior to know how to effectively and directly deal with aggression each day so it doesn't turn against the individual in psychosomatic conditions or go outward into senseless violence. The warrior of the modern day is like the warrior of old—aggression is a tool of natural living that can be utilized to directly deal with one's environment in a way that promotes one's own survival and the survival of one's community. As Moore and Gillette say, "Like all repressed archetypes, it goes underground, eventually to resurface in the form of emotional and physical violence, like a volcano that has lain dormant for centuries with the pressure gradually building up the magma chamber. If the Warrior is an instinctual energy form, then it is here to stay. And it pays to face it."[5] In our modern world, repression and unconscious acting out are the normal ways of expressing aggression, but the artful use of aggression is rare.

If we look, we can find models for conscious use of aggression. For example, in Zen archery, the archer works on her consciousness and becomes so aware of the target that she feels one with it. Only at this moment is the arrow released. The goal is not to hit the bull's eye but to be in an elevated state of consciousness. One psychological exercise with aggression is to

---

[5] Robert Moore and Douglas Gillette, *King, Warrior, Magician, Lover*, p. 75.

first identify that the person you want to confront is a part of you. Only once you become one with her do you confront her. The art of dealing with real and intense feelings needs to be taught, practiced, and mastered. Many of the teens I work with know more about operating a rifle than living with their feelings.

Here are some concrete steps to take when working with your own or someone else's violent feelings:

1. Set up the situation for everyone's physical safety. If you are working with your own violent feelings, find a place where you can let them out safely, where you can scream and be noisy. If you want to hit something, find a chair, mattress, pillow, or something you won't regret later that you broke, or that was so hard you end up injuring yourself. Many times I have seen clients who came in because they were tired of breaking their favorite china or guitar, or were tired of slamming their fists into walls and breaking their hands.

2. If you are working with yourself or with a client as a therapist, notice any small hurts. Serious injuries give lots of warning signals before they happen. For example, if you start moving with a client and they bump you and it hurts, stop and focus on this. Next, help the person express directly the part that could be hurtful. It is never necessary to wait until someone is physically hurt to bring out the part that wants to hurt, because it will always signal itself in small ways. This principle also holds true when working with yourself—if you hurt yourself when expressing anger and rage, stop and focus on this. Whom do you want to hurt? If it is yourself, find out why. If it is someone else, express this in drama or movement or be direct with the person. Process rather than damage or repress.

3. Fill out violence in a multi-channeled manner. One of the main causes of physical violence in relationships is the inability to express aggression verbally. Those who only talk need to move and use fantasy around aggression. Those who can only respond physically need to visualize and verbalize. Almost

everyone could use more awareness of the feelings in their body while they are angry.

4. We all need to teach ourselves, or be taught, to remain aware of different levels of signals simultaneously. Specifically this means we need to be able to stay in contact both with the part that wants to hurt, and with the part that doesn't want to hurt and cares about the other person. This is martial arts training—can you in your fury remember that this is your wife or husband or lover or friend or child you feel like hurting, but don't really want to hurt?

Often in people who are abusive, this dual awareness has never been modeled. Many of us had parents who couldn't stay aware when they were angry. Consciousness during anger takes practice.

5. People who can express their feelings are often limited to one major feeling in a particular area of their personality. They can cry but not get angry, or get angry but not express hurt. Expressing all of the feelings present prevents violence to oneself and others. Those feelings not allowed to come out directly come out indirectly and are potentially far more hurtful.

6. When you are angry, begin to develop awareness about situations and people with whom you are really angry. Much violence is a result of people taking out lifetimes of stored anger on others. The skilled individual presses herself to learn how much anger is related to the present, and how much to past situations and people evoked by the current person. The skilled person learns appropriate outlets for anger based in the present, and for the past anger that the present brings up.

7. If you are highly trained in how to deal with your anger, you care about how much anger and violence the other person can take, and are sensitive to this feedback. Some people can take lots of anger—they are physically and emotionally available. To give someone more aggression than they can defend against is potentially abusive. For others, one drop of anger is all they can take. for some, receiving anger in the right amount can be useful. The Zen master taps his students with his or her

stick on the shoulder to wake them up to their true nature, or may even shout at them. The point is that with awareness of the other, anger sent towards that person may be useful to them, and without awareness of who the other is, and what their feedback is, the anger may be abusive.

8. It is extremely important for therapists to work on their own aggression as well as help others. The therapist's genuine openness to people and all of their parts can make clients feel as if they have finally found a place to process their angry feelings. Whether you are a therapist or simply adopting this role, it is important to learn to move fluidly from supporting aggression to reacting by helping to set limits around it. If you are highly skilled in working with anger, you can give accurate feedback to help the client move closer and closer to the bull's eye. The skilled therapist knows that sometimes people can only learn about anger through a relationship encounter with the therapist. A skilled therapist knows how to make sure that both the client and the therapist come out of the work in better shape than they went in. The therapist who is highly skilled in anger work knows that words and theories aren't enough, because clients will see right through the contradictory signals if you aren't genuine in the work. Work on aggression includes setting limits and speaking up when you are scared.

9. Therapists need to know how to defend themselves in anger work. They should know that they may be physically attacked, and have some training in how to physically defend themselves. They should know that they need to create safety, for example, by telling someone who is really dangerous that they have to sit in their chair and not get out and instead work on their anger verbally. They need to know movement techniques for safely expressing anger physically, and to know their own physical limits.

As a therapist you never know when you need to be prepared for aggression. One time I was working with a woman in her sixties whom I had met for the first time. She was telling me a dream when she suddenly leaped across the room and began to choke me. I was so shocked that I yelled, "Sit down," and she did. We worked on that dream and all the violence in it for the next many weeks. I learned from this to be ready for attack, and to trust my instant and instinctual response. Readiness to deal with violence is important training for anybody working in this area.

AGGRESSION IN TEENAGERS

Teenagers who have been victimized by violence tend to turn against all authority. I have seen more teenage boys with authority figure problems than any other problem. Here's a typical scenario. A boy causes trouble in school, or is in trouble with the law. His unconscious aggression is expressed through beating up other teenagers, or swearing at or hitting teachers. In most cases, the boy's parents couldn't model constructive expression of aggressive feelings. In many cases, his parents were physically abusive to him or to each other. Another common cause is that the parents are alcoholic and vacillate between passive aggression and becoming drunk and violent.

Teenage boys need help learning to express their aggression in ways that don't hurt others, and help developing their own internal authority figures. Learning to express feelings verbally is also immensely helpful. I remember one boy who came to therapy because he was so angry that his family was afraid he might kill someone. When I introduced him to my punching bag, he suddenly found an outlet that worked, and became almost immediately a more relaxed, happy human being. He didn't want to hurt anyone—he was just a volcano looking for a place to explode, a boy who came from a family that was always making him angry and then forbade any expression of anger. After a few sessions, we both agreed he was not a danger to anyone, but he wanted to come back anyway. He worked through his anger so that he now had several non-dangerous ways of releasing it. He was thrilled, and felt much better about himself. People love feeling alive in ways that have been forbidden to them.

This basic scenario of finding the right channel for express-ing aggression, and then helping teenagers integrate these tools into their daily lives, has worked for me with hundreds of adolescents. Once the aggression comes out, we often have work to do around who is making them angry. Many of these boys come from single-parent families where the memory of their fathers is mostly defined through their mothers' hatred, or maybe they don't know their fathers at all. I worked with one boy who hadn't seen his father since the father left the family when the boy was very young. When the father attempted to reconnect with the boy in his teens, the mother could only say all the horrible things the father had once done. The father had succeeded in turning his life around, but the mother was too angry with him to admit this. The teenager was deprived of a potential model and father figure, and was also furious at the mother. He could have used that male model of how to turn around being a troublemaker, but the mom sabotaged all attempts at reconnection. The most we could do in therapy was acknowledge the teenager's feelings, and reassure him that in four or five years he would be old enough to reconnect on his own.

In his book on men healing themselves, Jed Diamond talks about boys without role models: "Sociological studies of delin-quent boys indicate that a high percentage of them come from families in which either there is no father in the household, or the father is on hand but abusive or violent. Cross cultural anthropological studies suggest that violent behavior is often characteristic of male adolescents and adults whose fathers were absent or played a small role in their sons' early rearing."[6]

When I ask teenage boys who won't listen to authority fig-ures what they want to be when they grow up, the answer is almost always something like a policeman, or a marine sergeant. Somehow they know they need to be able to create an inner authority in relation to their own aggression. They know

---

[6] Ted Diamond, *The Warrior's Journey Home*, p. 198.

that discipline and aggression need to be tied together to be a modern-day warrior, but where are they to get such training? For many of them the best option they know is military service or a police academy.

We need other kinds of training centers to help teenagers master their aggression. To hit the bull's eye with one's aggression, one must have all of oneself accessible—the one who can lose control and the one who can maintain control, not just one part or the other. When one part is split off, it victimizes the person. Bullies may taunt the one whose aggression is split off, or he may be violent towards others. When a boy feels powerless, learning about his internal authority, which can help him face the bullies, usually changes the situation. When one's internal control figure is underdeveloped or split off, teachers, judges, police, and social workers get pulled in to model authority. A boy who grows up without an authority figure will create authorities in the environment, usually by provoking trouble, even while denying that he would ever listen to anybody. There is wisdom in creating in your environment parts of yourself you need to work on, because then you have models. Through not listening, adults in the environment become increasingly authoritative. This cycle can go on until the teenager meets someone who can model fair authority and challenge him to develop his own inner authority.

PREVENTING VIOLENCE IN THE SCHOOLS

Every time there is an incident of school violence, great shock reverberates. Each year there are growing numbers of shootings in the schools. These are terrible tragedies that shake our basic foundations around safety for our children. The African American community has been especially helpful in pointing out that the focus on the schools now is important but also brings up pain in their community about how little attention has been given to violence that has been happening to their youth for so many years. They have also pointed out that racial hatred has played a part in some of the killings.

In most of the killings, there were many warning signs that were ignored by parents, fellow students, teachers, and administrators. Several of the young people had talked openly about going on a rampage. Most had been buying and stockpiling weapons. In both the Thurston school in Oregon and the Columbine school in Colorado, the boys had been busy making bombs.

The first step in preventing school violence is to take threats seriously. For a short time after a violent incident, schools may take extreme measures of caution. For example, a local elementary school student pointed his finger at another student and was suspended. This kind of overreaction isn't helpful. However, many other students since who have talked about killings or who have brought weapons to school, have been sent for professional help and evaluation and sometimes removed from the schools until they are considered safe to return. In one incident that didn't get reported to the news media, an elementary school child brought a loaded pistol to his classroom. A friend told the teacher, and potential disaster was avoided.

While this is the most immediate action to take to prevent violence, it is equally important to look at interventions in the schools so that we never reach the point where children are ready to kill at school. All of the work we have talked about in this book is based on changing how individuals, families, and systems deal with anger to help prevent violence to self and others. Before homicides at schools became common, suicide was already epidemic. Violence has been a problem in the schools for a long time, and only now is it getting the attention it deserves.

The second principle to avoid school violence is to pay attention to young people who seem especially hurt or are hurtful to others. The quiet, depressed, isolated, troubled male student too often ends up violent in the schools, especially if he has been put down at school. In the Columbine shootings, two members of the "Trenchcoat" group were responsible for the shootings. It turns out that the "jocks," a group with which the

Trenchcoat group had had conflicts, had beaten up some of these youth, humiliated them repeatedly, and threatened to kill them. Part of what these boys did comes out of a rage released by revenge. While there was likely a great deal of hurt and violence present in these young people long before these school incidents, such humiliations can push some youth over the edge. Schools need to watch out for scenes like this and work with them. Both the youth who are hurt and outcast and the popular students who put them down need counseling.

The third principle is to do conflict work between groups having conflicts, which happens in every school. School officials need to be trained in helping groups work on their issues. For example, I worked with two groups of girls who were fighting so intensely that many had dropped out of the class. After a few hours of conflict work, they were able to express what they didn't like about the other group and talk about how each group had been hurt by the other group. A big breakthrough came when the leaders of each group talked about their home lives. Both had been through recent parental divorces, and in this experience they found a common ground. I heard later that they had chosen each other to work together on a project.

The main skills in this kind of conflict work are to make both sides feel welcome, to make sure both sides get to speak, to focus on feeling issues, and to help both groups eventually find common ground. A good facilitator will notice when emotional moments occur in the discussion, and help the young people to focus on these as soon as they come up. Moments like this that are skipped over tend to lead to escalation. Another important part of this work is to get the young people to try to switch sides and become more fluid in their awareness. For example, let's say I am working with a group of young boys who mostly like working on computers, and a group of athletes. The computer group is called the "nerds" and the other group the "jocks." The "nerds" talk about how they feel put down by being called nerdy, and that they feel horrible for just being smart. Suddenly a jock talks about how *he* feels put down. People assume he is not intelligent just because he is interested in sports. An alert facilitator might see if the jock who feels put down will come stand for a moment on the side of those who put him down. When a nerd then begins to talk of his hatred of jocks, he has now become someone who puts *others* down, and can be asked to stand on *that* side. This is one way to help the young people see that these are roles that they all occupy at different times. It begins to break up some of the polarizing, and allows people to start seeing common ground.

The fourth principle is to create opportunities for young people to talk about how they feel about school violence and other issues as they come up. In many of the schools in my area, teachers have talked to the young people about what is being done to ensure safety in the schools, but students are seldom asked how they feel about the violence. As a therapist in private practice, I had several young people come in to talk about how afraid they were to go to school with all of the violence they had heard about in other schools. Students need to be able to talk about their fears together and to have times to talk about how they feel about other school topics such as homework, boredom or interest level in their subjects, social pressures, being popular or not, academic pressure, and what it is like to be young people in these times. Young people who can talk things out are much less likely to act out with violence. Those who don't speak up may find relief in just listening to others. Teachers need to create atmospheres where young people are supported to bring out their hurt and anger. The more outlets for expression, the fewer potential bullets that fly. Students need to feel that their teachers care, that they can come to them and tell them who they feel frightened by at school, and what rumors they have heard.

The fifth principle is to have more counselors and social workers available in the schools. Many schools don't have counselors, and those that do often give the counselors so much work with scheduling and other tasks that it is rare for them to have any time for students' personal and emotional issues.

The sixth principle is that schools need to have trained facilitators lead open forums for the whole student body. In an open forum, different issues can come up and be focused on. For example, a school might have a forum on racism, sexism, homophobia, violence, or popularity issues.

The seventh and final principle is that all students should be taught basic conflict work techniques from the elementary grades on. Students need to learn to facilitate conflict between individuals, groups, and at meeting of the whole school. Learning to deal with conflict in life is a key part of staying healthy, and needs to be taught in the schools, just as health classes are. The Process Work community offers such training, as do other schools of facilitation.

While there are no guarantees around school violence, if schools will take these steps, the amount of violence will be greatly reduced. Violence is a call to attention, through which young people ask for help with the intensity of their experiences.

AGGRESSION IN ADULTS

Aggression is a problem for people of all ages, not just for teenagers. School violence can't be addressed without also looking at the role anger plays in the students' home lives. I remember working with a couple on a common relationship problem. The woman complained that she was losing interest in her husband—he just wasn't exciting to her. When they came into the office, I could see why. He acted distant, cold, and bored. When she challenged him to respond, he couldn't, so she continued to make plans to leave him. At this point, I asked him to show me what he was like on the job. He was tough, active, related, and aggressive. I asked him to be this way with his wife, even for a minute. He simply could not. Then we discovered that the man's father had been a monster at home, beating up the man's mother. This man was never aggressive at home, fearing he would become like his father. Now, he needed to learn to stand up to his wife's challenges, not like his father the abuser, but in a productive way. I often tell people in situations like this that maybe they need one drop of their father in them, sort of like cayenne in soup. The father was like two full jars of cayenne and made everyone sick, but a few drops could add spice to the soup and the marriage. In fact, when the edge to an abusive figure is processed fully, I have never seen a person be anything like their abusive parent. This client was willing to change because he desperately wanted his marriage to survive.

A difficult and a wonderful challenge in most cases of aggression is that the patterns and problems have been passed down over generations. The exciting challenge is to finally grab the horse by its reins and turn the pattern around. In our world today, the amount of aggressive stimulation has increased dramatically, while appropriate outlets have decreased, especially as physical labor decreases in the average person's life. Pediatrician and psychiatrist Michael Rotherenberg states that the average child has seen 18,000 murders on television by the time he or she graduates from high school (*Wildfire Magazine*, Vol. 4, No. 1). There are plenty of models for dangerous ways to be aggressive, but few that show how to live creatively and productively with one's aggression.

If we help one person change, that person impacts everyone around her. In a small town, counseling centers serve as recycling plants for potentially toxic wastes. If people have a productive outlet for their aggression, violence against others decreases and aggression can be recycled into personal power, creativity, relatedness, and assertiveness. Many psychological approaches have done a great deal to help people with their aggression. Gestalt has helped people express aggression verbally, while bioenergetic approaches have made pounding on pillows and other physical releases an accepted part of therapy. Reality-oriented therapies helped people develop some sense of the consequences of their actions and helped people become their own authority figures. Process-oriented psychology builds on these approaches through working with what is already happening, following and amplifying it.

For example, a woman once told me that she was not angry that her husband died young, leaving her a single parent. While she was telling me that she was done mourning, I noticed that her fists were clenched. I asked her if I could put my hands on top of her fists. She began to push against them, and then to smack at my hands. She was soon screaming and crying about how her husband left her just when their life was going well. This wealth of feeling all emerged simply from following her signal of clenched fists, and then letting what needed to happen unfold.

A similar example is of a woman who had had a car accident. Someone had hit her parked car and driven away without stopping. The woman felt that she was really upset about the incident, but that she couldn't get in touch with her rage. When I asked her who could deal with the hit-and-run driver, she said her ex-boyfriend could. We began to play out the roles; I acted like the hit-and-run driver. This woman who could barely admit that she was upset suddenly pushed me against the wall and said, "Don't you ever treat someone like that again." She was powerful and effective. In this case, the signal we followed and amplified was the character of the ex-boyfriend, which unfolded into a part of the woman that could stand up for herself. Once a figure is accessed, the next step is integration. This woman and I talked about several people with whom she needed to be more firm to stop them from "running her over." This was particularly true in relationship to her ex-boyfriend.

Accidents are one way that we become the victims of aggression. For people's safety, it is very important to work with the process behind accidents. One way to do this is by reenacting the scene and finding the meaning in it. For example, a car that spun out of control hit the car of a woman client of mine. We worked on identifying a part in her that might need to be more out of control, since she came from a rigid family system. As this woman began to experiment with being less controlled, the terror she had felt since the accident lessened. One of the fascinating elements of working with people on violence is that people move from having their aggressiveness cause trouble to having it become the fuel for their creative spirit and personal power.

Many people are addicted to aggression, either to the adrenaline rush of getting angry, regardless of its effects in their life, or to the emotional relief of being able to express feeling. Particularly for men, aggression is easier to express than hurt or fear, which often lies beneath aggression. Aggression that is an addiction must be seen, and addressed, as such, with all of its potential for self-destruction and destruction of intimate relationships. Another key element in using aggression constructively is to create clear boundaries. Not standing for a personal boundary often leads to aggression and violence, which can be prevented when people learn to make and respect boundaries. Other issues, too, need to be addressed to stop relationship violence, including sexism, rank, and power differences. We will explore these further in Chapter XIV.

CHAPTER V

SUICIDE: PROCESS THE STATE AND LET THE BODY LIVE

Suicide has become a nationwide epidemic, particularly among teenagers. In my small town I see many people contemplating suicide. While suicide used to be quite scary for me to work with, I now find it most of the time a straightforward, manageable situation. There are two significant parts to the work. The short-term plan helps the person move out of their suicidal state, while longer-term treatment focuses on helping them make changes to resolve the situation that pushed them into a suicidal state. Moving someone out of the suicidal state is usually less difficult than resolving the situation that led to the state in the first place.

TYPES OF SUICIDAL CLIENTS

There are three basic types of suicidal clients. In acute cases, a person is reacting to one or several incidents that pushed them over the edge into suicidal feelings. Such a person may have been previously stable. Possible cases of this sort include the teenager who breaks up with a loved one; the couple who have a huge fight and one leaves; the person who is unexpectedly fired; the young person who comes home and discovers that her parents are separating, or a person who finds that vicious rumors about them are circulating. These and similar one-time crises can push people to the brink of suicide.

The second group of suicidal people includes those in longer-term unhappy situations. In these cases, suicide is contemplated as a way out, a cry for help, or possibly as a way to get even. For example, I have seen several teenagers who are so unhappy with what is truly an awful home situation that they are suicidal either until the family makes major changes, or until the teenager is placed in a new family situation. This can also be true of marital relationships. For example, I have worked with a number of women who have been severely battered. Their self-esteem has hit such a rock-bottom place that the only way they feel they can escape is through suicide. I have worked with several teenage girls who were both suicidal and anorexic. They had been through all kinds of treatment programs. Each caregiver had a different theory about the psychodynamics of these young women's personalities. In several of these cases very practical solutions were required— one girl needed a new home, another to re-establish contact with a father who had left the home. Often other families are willing to reach out and help each other through tough times, especially when teenagers are involved.

Communities used to do a better job of absorbing troubled people. The number of troubled people on the streets is a modern symptom of the breakdown of community.

Even in smaller towns, people are beginning to fall through the cracks, and the number of homeless people is growing, although more slowly than in cities. The need for community is a serious longing, and not feeling part of a community pushes many people into despair. I recently worked with a suicidal young woman who repeatedly said she felt she didn't belong to any community, had never really felt a part of her family, and saw no other solution but to kill herself. Her work has been to discover why she doesn't belong, and to find a way to belong. Modern life is full of stories of people lying wounded and dying in the middle of a city because nobody stops to help them. In most small towns, my experience has been if someone is lying on the street hurt, the main problem is going to be getting the ambulance technicians through the crowds who are trying to help.

Once when I was in India, I asked a taxi driver about how people respond to traffic accidents. He said that before ambulances arrive, everyone has stopped and done all they can, often even taking injured people to the hospital. This may not be the best medical intervention, but on a feeling level, it is an amazing statement that we are all part of one big family. This kind of feeling is missing in many of our cities and suburbs in the United States.

The third group of suicidal people includes individuals whose personal psychological problems are quite severe. These people may have been hospitalized previously as a result of suicide attempts, and they may be suffering from severe and chronic depression. These chronic patterns are more difficult to work with, but it is often possible to help people in these states.

TREATMENT APPROACHES

There are certain common elements to treating all three types of suicidal people, and certain differences based on whether the situation is acute or chronic. In acute crises, the most important intervention is that the therapist be emotionally real and genuinely able to convey availability during this crisis period. I remember a teenage boy who was in a terrible crisis in his relationship. He couldn't find anyone he felt he could talk to. I was real with him—I told him that I liked him, which was true, that I didn't want him to kill himself, and that I had helped lots of teenagers through this kind of problem. I asked him if he would still want to kill himself if he got some help with his relationship. He said, of course not, so I promised I would try to help him, and told him that I was also available to work with the two of them as a couple. Doing couples therapy with teenagers is very important. Not only does it help them with their specific problems, but it also conveys that their problems are important. Many parents make light of teenage relationships, but they need to be taken seriously. They involve love, sex, feeling good about oneself, and the positive potential of life. When an adolescent relationship falls apart, deep wounds open, often from early hurts that may not have been touched upon for years. In the case of this teenager, the simple intervention of saying, "I care and will help you with what's bothering you" was enough to bring him out of the suicidal state. He didn't want to die; he just wanted the emotional pain to stop. Besides offering caring and love, there are a few other basic steps I recommend with suicidal people at the crisis level. I increase my availability, including giving them my home phone number. I often ask for a commitment that they will not attempt suicide while working with me, and tell them that if I can't help I will send them to someone who can. Sometimes I draw up an agreement with them, saying that I will work with them and that they must commit to working with me for a certain number of weeks and promise not to attempt suicide during that time. Clients have always kept their part of our agreements. However, I want to warn against making contracts a set program. For some people, an intervention like this provides temporary structure that may be necessary. However, some therapists make suicide prevention contracts a requirement for therapy, which may cost some people their lives.

I worked with one woman in her twenties whose mother convinced her to come to therapy for depression. For weeks she told me that she was going to kill herself, and refused to be hospitalized. She insisted that she couldn't stand living, and that it was her fate to be dead. We went as far as we could in working with her issues. Behind her depression was a deep spirituality; behind her view of death was the detachment of a Buddha. At one point, she told me that she needed to be working with a woman, and she switched therapists. I kept up with her progress, and learned that she eventually gave up her suicidal longings. If either of us, as her therapists, had insisted that she make a contract not to kill herself, she would have quit therapy. She needed the option of knowing she could get out of her life, which gave her the freedom to begin thinking about staying on the planet. Her interest in living needed to unfold at her own pace.

Talking to one part of the person about the other part that wants to kill itself may be helpful. For example, I may point out that some part of the person wants to die, such as some old way of being or relating or feeling, but that this shouldn't be confused with killing the physical body, which is a total and permanent action. Talking about how one part needs to die, but the organism gets confused and wants to kill the whole person, is useful in part because it confirms the rightness of feeling suicidal. There is often something right about feeling this way, as some major change is needed. But confusing change and death can be a tragic mistake.

I remember one woman who was facing this dilemma where a part attempted to kill the whole. The woman and her husband had come for therapy many years earlier. The husband called me one day in a panic, saying that his wife had just slit her wrists and was all right physically, but not mentally. I said to bring her in. After talking for quite a while, we couldn't really understand what had motivated the suicide attempt. I suggested a powerful intervention, saying, "Let's reenact the suicide here, in a safe role play, to find out what is actually going on." She pretended to cut her wrists, and went into a deep trance while lying on the floor. When she came out of the trance, she told the following story. She was once a very creative artist with powerful spiritual visions that she translated into art. She had given this part of her life up to be a more practical person. The woman said, after the trance, "I am now committed to doing my art. I know the kinds of things I need to be drawing." In her case, the suicide attempt was an effort to kill the part that kept her on Earth in ordinary ways, and the artist was trying to be born.

Here we can see that the potentially dangerous part of the self may contain the seed of healing. This woman needed support to pursue her art. She is doing beautiful work and has not had further suicide attempts.

In terms of systems that need to change before people stop being suicidal, I remember several teenagers who wanted out of their families. They lived in homes where the parents were not providing positive attention. Instead, they had alcoholic or explosive fathers lurking in the background, or mothers who wouldn't let go and treated the teenagers as if they were grade school children. In these cases, the feeling of wanting to leave was right for the suicidal teenager, but the leaving needed to happen in a more constructive way. These teenagers needed help to grow past their families in a healthy way instead of taking a permanently destructive way out.

Sometimes if the family is highly dysfunctional, the teenager will get out any way they can. If the system can't change, a new living setting is much better than a coffin. In other cases, family functioning can improve enough to help the teenager who has felt suicidal. I remember one family where the teenager was expressing a need for his father to be around more. The mother felt the same. She was depressed but could not express her needs. The father in this family had actually felt unwanted and thus drew back from involvement. Over time, as the father became more involved with his family, fishing and camping trips replaced the teenager's forays into feeling suicidal and depressed.

One key factor to be aware of in working with suicide prevention in teens is the whole issue of sexual identity. Many therapists report that up to 50% of the teenage suicide attempts they see come from teens who are either gay, lesbian, bisexual, or transgendered, or worried that they might be. Homophobia is rampant among teens and, for many teens, the struggle around their sexual identity in the context of such intolerance can be so painful that they contemplate or attempt suicide. These problems call both for personal therapy and for addressing the bigger social problem of homophobia in the schools. Individual therapy often includes helping the young person clarify where their sexual identity lies, and then helping them deal with their family, friends, and the intolerant culture that they are living in.

Support groups can also be very helpful in this area. Support groups are available for parents and families of gay, lesbian, bisexual, and transgendered youth, and for youth whose sexual identity falls out of the mainstream heterosexual model. In terms of social change, it is important for therapists to train school staff in how to create more openness to diversity of all sorts, including race, religion, class, gender, sexual identity, and so on. Teachers and counselors need to be trained and empowered to act when they see young people being made fun of or harassed for their sexual identity. They also need to be trained in how to have discussions with their classes where issues of diversity can be talked about openly. One of the central issues behind suicide and homicide in schools is how many young people feel put down for being different, for being who they are. Some of us in the Process Work community are busy trying to devise curricula to educate teachers and students about how to work on diversity issues together. Through therapy and through changes in the schools, we will begin to reverse this dangerous trend of growing suicide because of sexual identity concerns.

The third group of suicidal people includes those with a chronic history of depression and suicidal feelings and/or suicide attempts. Often these people have been hospitalized at least once for their condition. There are differences between working with someone like this and working with someone from the other groups. First, these people often need more help organizing the basics in their lives, including housing, money, work, and company. In terms of Maslow's hierarchy of needs, these people need support for the basics of life as well as help to work on their existential crises. A good therapist needs to be as available to help someone find housing as to hear his or her deepest concerns.

Another difference is that there are specific interventions to bring a person out of a deep or chronic depression. For the best guide to working with severe mental illness, see Arnold Mindell's *City Shadows*. If a person is in an extreme state of depression from which they cannot communicate about their psyche or reflect on their state, we need to help free the person from this state so that they can regain self-awareness. One intervention that is highly successful is to take over the process and do the depression better than the depressed person does. When working with a severely depressed person, it is important for the therapist to pick up those moments when she genuinely feels like giving up.

For example, I saw a woman who had been both a great mother to her children and successful at her work. Suddenly, she became very depressed, suicidal, and lost all interest in life. She was brought to me after being hospitalized, which had had little effect. At one point in the work I felt like giving up. I had tried everything, was working really hard, and she wouldn't budge. I told her I was ready to give up. At this point she was able to instruct me in how to live, saying "You can't give up, you have too much going for you, life is good, even if you have failures, you have to keep going." She was giving me the data I needed to know how to help rekindle her interest in life. In working with someone in such a state, small steps are big progress. After the session, she wanted to pick some of the blackberries growing around my office. This was progress in terms of her being interested in life again. Again, it is important to emphasize that working with someone who has had repeated bouts of depression takes time, patience, and an ability to see incremental steps of improvement.

As the gaps in mental health services grow, we see more and more people with serious mental problems at our clinic. Psychiatric hospitals release people with a prescription to help keep them from getting worse, but people still need assistance with the transition to ordinary life. Halfway houses that help people work their way back into mainstream life are simply not doing the job, since funding has been cut, and only the most severely disturbed or those with enough personal wealth to hire the daily care they need get help. Also, there are not enough services for the poor, and those who don't qualify for government programs but can't afford private daily care have to go somewhere. Often they end up in smaller private clinics, using either their few resources or family insurance coverage. Even private insurance often does not provide coverage for the number of sessions the person may need each week. Still, the private clinic, particularly in a small town, may be the only place available to assist people, and those of us who work in private clinics must be ready to help more severely disturbed people. People in more extreme states often frighten therapists.

THE CITY SHADOW CONCEPT

People who are in unusual states carry and express the more shadowy parts of all of us. Mindell develops this concept in *City Shadows*.[7] Jungian psychology defined the shadow part of the individual, which is that part of ourselves that we don't want to look at, the hidden part of us that only comes up in our dreams. Mindell takes this concept further and says that cities too have shadows. People in extreme states represent this city shadow. Like a dream that keeps reminding of us of these disavowed parts, people in extreme states are living representations of the parts the rest of us split off. We tend to be frightened of people with various conditions because they carry parts of ourselves that scare us. Working with people in extreme states is difficult for the therapist because it brings up parts, such as deep depression, mania, or other out-of-control parts, that the therapist has not yet processed himself or herself. Once someone works through these parts, meeting them in others can be challenging and exciting. Part of the reason that we as a society want people in unusual states medicated is so we won't have to face the parts of ourselves that these people carry.

Simply being open to processing an extreme state without having to pull the person out of it can be tremendously healing for both therapist and client. When people have come far enough out of their extreme states to communicate, I some-

---

7 Arnold Mindell, *City Shadows,* p. 165

times thank them for being willing to work on these pieces, these shadowy parts, which belong to all of us. As we build a more compassionate and accepting world, more people will want to stay on the planet and fewer will want to end their lives. Suicide cannot be eliminated as a problem until we make the world a more humane, loving place to be, where people can go though the downs of life without falling off, over the edge of despair and having nobody to toss them a rope. People need safety nets, that is, people and places that support them to reorganize their lives and heal after they have been pushed over the edge. I see a need for places in the city and the country where people can go to rest, exercise, do physical labor such as gardening, and get counseling. Such places should provide freedom and be stigma free, unlike psychiatric hospitals. Such a refuge could help people with the changes that are trying to happen through suicide, assisting them through the death of an old way of being and the discovery of a new one.

CHAPTER VI

THE CHANGING WORLD OF RELATIONSHIPS

In this chapter, we will begin to explore some of the relationship issues that are specifically highlighted in small towns.

WOMEN'S AND MEN'S LIBERATION COMES TO SMALL TOWNS

The impact that shifting sexual identity roles has on relationships is behind many relationship difficulties everywhere, and is especially clear in small towns. Small town people are caught between conservative attitudes that support traditional sexual stereotypes and the values of feminism and men's liberation influential in all parts of the culture. For example, many women try to force themselves to fit into old roles they no longer believe in. This attempt to fit an old role often comes out in sexual problems. Many women in couples sessions describe how they don't pay attention to their own pleasure at all, but lie back and hope the man will get it over with soon. Sex is still seen as part of their wifely duty. It is obvious from the outside that this conflict of interest is causing the sexual difficulties, but simple solutions don't work because the cultural conditioning goes so deeply.

On the other hand, their bodies rebel and refuse to perform, regardless of what their minds think a good wife should do. I have been able to intellectually connect with many couples to help them understand that if they can make their sex lives more mutually satisfying they will both get more of what they want, yet the resistance I come across is enormous. It is clear that what I am saying goes against everything they have learned about what a man is supposed to do. Many men still have a basic belief that their satisfaction is part of the wedding agreement, a trade-off that compensates them for working hard in the world. On the other hand, when I have encouraged women to try to get more for themselves, and to actually say "no" when they don't want to have sex, what often comes up is fear of losing their man. Many women have been taught by their culture that being themselves means they have to be alone, so it is better to keep quiet about their own needs. It is very difficult to get either party to change—both are bound by their cultural conditioning.

I also see this in emotional patterns. Many men are ready to develop more of their emotional selves, but are up against old conditioning that says men don't show their feelings. Rather than expressing their deep needs and consciously dealing with their feelings, many men turn to alcohol. They drink either to deaden their feelings, or to knock out the feeling inhibitor long enough to release some feelings. Having and being with one's feelings is difficult enough; sharing them with significant others in a communicative way is a whole different, additional task. It is extremely difficult to go against cultural norms and follow one's own needs and path in relationships.

Women in small towns feel especially inhibited about expressing their anger in intimate relationships. In *The Anger Trap*, Elizabeth Weiss clearly identifies some of the reasons women are afraid to express anger. "A woman does not hide her anger because of an unsupportive partner alone. Society pressures women to be silent. While men and women are equally capable of expressing their anger, for centuries there has been a taboo about women expressing anger."[8] She goes on to say, "Many women have this 'don't make waves' attitude.

---

[8] Elizabeth Weiss, *The Anger Trap*, p. 15.

Their entire personalities are based on being 'nice.' They fear anger will kill love and most of us cannot live without love." Weiss defines this kind of love as neurotic love, which will be killed by anger, as opposed to a healthier love. "But this is not love at all; it is neurotic dependency. This type of relationship will probably be destroyed, despite all of our attempts, because strain is inevitable. Meaningful love—love which lasts—is actually strengthened by anger. It reunites a couple. Indeed, a certain amount of anger is necessary for intimacy."[9] Weiss points out that women's restrictions and blocks around anger are culturally based. Women's liberation, with its emphasis on assertiveness training, is changing this dynamic.

We can clearly see sex role conflicts played out in small towns where there is much support for following traditional norms. Even in small, conservative areas, ideas popular in the rest of the culture sufficiently penetrate people's thinking to make them question and challenge traditional ways of being. We see another level of sorting out sex roles on the job. In small towns, many men feel that they, as the main breadwinners, have the final say in decisions. Many women, in couples and family sessions, defer to their husband's judgment as head of the household, when in fact their actual situation does not fit the male breadwinner/female housekeeper model they are operating under. Often, the father works a traditional job at the mill or in a factory. The mother still does the cooking and cleaning and bulk of the child raising, but more often than not she also works outside the home. She cooks at a school, works at a mill, or has an office job, usually arranging her schedule so that she can be home for the children after school and in time to cook supper. Sometimes the woman makes more money than her husband, often without realizing that the power formulas are changing.

I once worked with a couple where the woman said to her husband that the game was over. She wasn't putting up with

---

[9] Elizabeth Weiss, *The Anger Trap*, p. 7.

doing all the work with the children and at home, while he hunted every weekend. She now brought more money into the family than he did. He said he wouldn't change the power structure and job structure, so she left him.

There are many women who say that not having to work outside the home is a dream come true, but this picture is changing rapidly. The number of women going back to school to develop or advance their careers is growing. The number of women who are earning as much as or more than their husbands, and who want to change the power structure, childcare arrangements, and other aspects of life, is growing. There are huge problems in the traditional sex role setup. A certain percentage of women feel repressed by being forced into a role that may or may not fit their personality. Many women are super-moms at home and work and also say that the man is the decision-maker and the head of the house. In the back of such an arrangement lurks enough resentment to tear the marriage apart. Also, the idea of dad as decision-maker is not practical if dad is never home. Many fathers work shifts where they may not see the children much during the workweek. The power in many of these families needs to shift to the mother, as she is the one who knows what is going on. If the father has the skills and interest in making the decisions, he may serve well as decision-maker, or the two may work jointly and cooperatively.

What makes most sense is that people divide power in a family based on their interests and skills, and in this way form a team. Otherwise, both parents end up stressed out and exhausted, and this exhaustion has consequences. As one woman said during a couples session, "Are you kidding? He expects all this and then I am supposed to want to have sex at night? All I want is some rest." In many cases, the raw anger and resentment that fueled much of the women's movement are present in small town psychology, but the changes in terms of status and recognition for women have not yet happened.

The women's movement could make great strides in small towns. Women need support for their feelings about sex roles, and support to translate these feelings into changes in their relationships that ensure better treatment. Men also need to be liberated. Many are exhausted and stressed from working many hours to make ends meet. Men often complain to me about being stuck into the role of disciplinarian when they get home from work. As one man said, I work all day and then come home and my wife has saved up all the things the children have done wrong. It's up to me to punish them, and I am always the bad guy. Men frequently complain that they are cast into the role of the heavy-handed one in terms of child raising, and that they then suffer from lack of closeness with their children. I have seen several couples where the man is about to leave because the woman is demanding more sexually or emotionally or both, and the man is too tired to do anything except collapse in front of the television. Men in small towns often feel terribly oppressed—by their jobs, and by the demands that they fit the cultural definition of the strong, unemotional, competent man. At home, these men switch and become the oppressors. Men and women's liberation is intimately connected; both need to occur. I have seen many men who need their female partners to become more and more liberated; the women are breaking trail for the men to follow in their own development.

I work with many men who are desperate to explore their inner lives and their emotional selves, for which they have little cultural support. Often men in this culture are tossed into their emotions when they come home one night to hear that their wife, seemingly out of nowhere, has packed her bags and announced she is leaving. I have seen the toughest men come into my office because they just can't stop crying. It's terribly sad. This is a difficult way for men to integrate their emotional side—like learning to swim by being thrown into deep water.

Many of the men I have worked with suffer because they also need time for the other parts of their lives. They are good husbands, good fathers, and feel like they are fighting to have independent selves who can go off with a friend for dinner, or hunting, or to have some time to think. Both men and women complain bitterly about the lack of time to live out all the parts of their life. The traditional role system around work, which has often come to mean two partners working, guarantees a minimum of communication time. One study measured how much time parents spend each day communicating with their children and found that it was only a few minutes. In trying to keep financially afloat, families make huge sacrifices in terms of quality time together.

For couples, the most common scenario for coming to a therapist is that one partner or the other is about to end the relationship either through walking away, or through going off with someone else. Usually women want therapy, and men will come along if their marriage is in jeopardy and they want to save it. The cultural conditioning for males in small towns is that you can fix anything yourself, whether it is your car or your marriage. The problem is that most men have had lots of training to fix cars, but when it comes to working out relationship problems, most haven't had enough training to do the equivalent of opening the car hood and looking at the engine. Often people wait until their relationships are in serious crisis and then want an instant fix. One way to support the rugged individualism present in small towns is to say that the skills people learn in therapy will help them work on their relationships more effectively at home.

Oftentimes, crises arise where we have to be willing to grow or face the more painful loss of our relationships. This is a classic choice that makes couples come to therapy—it is less painful to grow than to split up. Therapy is slowly becoming an "in thing" after many years of stigma. People come because they are in crisis, want more vitality in their relationships, or want to make progress on chronic problems. Again, much of what pushes people into crises is the lack of communication, and one of the areas where there is the least communication is in working out the conflict between people's real feelings and the gender roles they are supposed to play. Relationship crises are frightening for many reasons. They threaten the status quo of our lives. Suddenly we are in touch with parts of ourselves that we have may have been out of touch with our entire adult life, such as the fear of abandonment.

Once people are open to confronting and changing some of the gender roles they are living out, it is often very useful to help them explore roles and new balances that are more satisfying. I have seen relationships make huge changes when the man is open to doing some housecleaning, or starts sharing the childcare, or when the woman frees herself to take classes or to start asserting her needs in the relationship. Couples blossom when they begin to see that life can be a win-win situation, with both people getting the nourishment they need.

Sometimes when changes in sex roles are made, one person thinks they are really giving up a lot of power or benefits, but these changes can also be set up so that both people gain more of what they need. Couple dynamics are often set up as "either I am fulfilled or you are fulfilled. If we both need, there are no other places to fulfill our needs, so let's fight over the limited nourishment available." It is valuable in these situations to focus on human liberation, helping people contact more of their full selves and thus to live life more completely. We all have our own masculine and feminine sides, and both of these sides need to be supported to come out. Much of oppressing each other is because we forget that we are also the other. Sex roles are a way of saying, "this is who I am and this is who you are" but, especially in long-term relationships, who you are is also who I am. We tend to marry our secondary processes, particularly in the first half of life. We pick partners who carry parts of ourselves that we need to integrate, and with which we don't identify. When I picked a partner to marry, I was withdrawn from the world. I wanted to live in an isolated area, farm organically, and explore my spirituality. My wife had been remodeling houses and was extremely competent in the world. Over many years of marriage, we have become each other in this way. I have become much more competent in the world, while she has delved deeply into her spiritual development.

In many couples the men are learning to be more feeling, and the women are developing their ambition and wanting to be free of having to be feeling. All of this reflects the drive to wholeness. Jungian psychology says that each person has many different parts, including the masculine in women and the feminine in men. The path of wholeness means that we can't avoid developing in all areas simply because of our gender; rather, we need to embrace our whole selves. Oppression changes when we understand that whatever we oppress is also ourselves. When we realize that we suffer from lack of connection with our wholeness, then oppression has the potential to cease.

LEARNING TO SUPPORT EACH OTHER

Being a couple in the midst of a competitive society is difficult. One of the most complex ideas to communicate in couples work is that the couple is a system; like two people on a seesaw, whatever one does affects the other. The everyday competitive approach we use to relationships won't work, since one person on a seesaw can't win if the other one loses—the only way to have a good time is if a cooperative flow is happening.

Getting the relationship to plug into all the nourishment available from the environment, from each other, and from each individual's own self is not an easy procedure. Most of us are so busy avoiding and fighting and projecting that we forget we are hungry and that there are lots of blackberries nearby for both of us. I like working with couples on liberating both people by exploring alternatives that make them happier. For example, I have helped people re-arrange childcare arrangements to come up with solutions more satisfying to both. Usually the women have been doing it all. When the childcare is balanced out, men get to have more contact with their children, and women often have more energy, including more energy for the relationship itself. I have helped people find different balances around work, where the man works less at his job, but does more at home, and the woman gets out of the house more.

JOB CHANGES AND RELATIONSHIP HAPPINESS

Many people are stuck in jobs they hate or that make them sick. It is important to help people either to improve their situation, or to leave and find a better arrangement. Sometimes people really want to be running their own businesses. People have incredible skills that could be turned into money-making opportunities if necessary, and often they just need the encouragement and support to follow their dreams and become their own employers.

Simply put, when people are doing what they enjoy, life gets better. Many people enjoy working from home, which often helps couples balance work time and childcare time. Working from home is not a panacea. It can create problems where couples feel they have too much time together, but this can be worked with. Some people work best for others, where they don't have to bear the full pressure and responsibility of creating and running a business, but self-employment is an alternative worth exploring, especially for the many people who don't enjoy working at a job that doesn't interest them. People who are fulfilled with what they are doing are better partners. It is easy to blame lack of happiness on our mates, when in fact other parts of our lives actually need to change. Maybe we need to pay better attention to our physical health; maybe our work life is not fulfilling; maybe we need more outlets for our creativity, maybe we need more time to work on personal growth.

CULTURAL DEFINITIONS OF THE HAPPY COUPLE

A great danger for relationships is getting bound up in the culturally accepted idea of what a couple should be. In many cases this model emphasizes the well-being of the couple over the well-being of the individual. I have seen many couples for whom "unto death do us part" becomes a reality. These couples may have tried unsuccessfully to separate, or may have stayed together and suffered their unhappiness with each other. Eventually one partner develops a life-threatening illness, which either changes the relationship, or one person leaves or the ill partner dies.

One of the most difficult balances for couples to achieve is between coupling and individuality, that is, being able to be separate within the couple. Many people tend to feel guilty about their separate lives. In many couples, people tend to fall into a polarity. At one end of the spectrum is the couple where the wife is furious because she never sees the husband—when he is not working he is with the boys, and when not with the boys he is hunting or fishing. This is basically a non-relationship with a joint bank account. On the other end is a couple where the man is furious because he feels that in order to be a good husband and father he should be home all of the time he is not working. This man has given up all his hobbies and interests beyond the family. Secretly he longs for separation. Another example is a couple I saw where the woman met her husband, dropped out of school to be a housewife, and then became depressed. She needed to connect with her independent self that wanted to study.

As a culture, we are creating new models of relationship that include separation and divorce. I often tell couples to metaphorically divorce any time they feel like it, rather than waiting, letting issues build, and getting an actual divorce. In other words, it is important for each partner to feel free to drop being married at moments during the relationship. Little leavings prevent big ones. Parents need to structure their lives so they have time as a couple without their children. For some couples, having one or two nights a week to be together and focus on each other is very helpful. Children tend to dominate the parents' attention to the point that partners don't have time to focus on each other. One of the most common reasons that couples come in on the verge of divorce is that one or both feel that they no longer have intimate time together, only family time. Many couples give up feeding their relationship, thinking that they must devote time to the family. In the long run, however, too much time focusing only on the family may break up the family. This concept can be very difficult for couples; it is often helpful to remind them of what they used to enjoy together that they have given up since having children. It is not easy to find couple time, especially with all the demands on families, but it is essential—otherwise, the relationship becomes a neglected garden that may end up barren.

On the other hand, many couples find it useful to each take one night a week to act like they are single, feeling free to take a class or go to a movie with a friend. Working out these polarities within the context of a relationship saves people much suffering. One common pattern is that these needs for connection and independence are met by a cycling between polarities—get married, feel suffocated, get divorced, feel alone, get married, and so on. I try to help couples learn to respect themselves as a couple and also to nurture each other as individuals.

INDIVIDUAL WORK IN COUPLES THERAPY

When working with couples, it is often important to take a detour and work on the individual, since it is necessary to distinguish which issues belong to the couple and which are more individual. Let's say a couple has chronic fights. We might observe that one partner is angry no matter what happens. This may indicate that the person could use some individual therapy at this time. This person might still be so angry with one of their parents that their partner will continue to be their psychological punching bag until this anger can be worked through. By transferring it onto the partner, anger can be partially processed, but most relationships cannot survive years with one partner as the punching bag.

In some therapeutic theories, doing individual work in the middle of couples work is viewed as harmful to the therapy, since individual work could dissipate the tension needed to move the couple through necessary changes. However, this is only true with certain couples. With others, in the background of couple problems lurks a well of anger, pain, blocked sexuality, or something that goes beyond the relationship. Whatever is in the background must move before the relationship can move. It can be useful to do individual work with the other partner watching, and then may go back to relationship work, bringing in the watcher's reactions. Other times it can be useful to see one partner separately for a while, and then go back to couples work.

Many therapists do not want to go back and forth between individual and couple focus, since it creates too much complexity in the therapeutic relationship. Process-oriented psychology trains therapists to maintain awareness while moving fluidly between individual and couple focus. For example, I often find that one member of a couple is lost in a trance state, caught in an old scenario that keeps them from being able to come into the present with their partner. In such a situation, I would take the person deep into their dreaming process to clear up the past incident that put them into the trance, and then they can be more present. Many of us are lost in a trance due to some nasty figure in our lives. Often one scene sticks in someone's mind and acts as the poisonous apple that the witch gives Sleeping Beauty to make her sleep.

These dream states most clearly appear in people who have a history of physical or sexual abuse. Imagine that John goes to touch Susan. Susan gets a frightened look on her face, her body shuts down, and despite loving John she can't open to him. Instead she is back in a scene where her father is sexually abusing her, and she is re-experiencing the terror. Other times Susan tries to come close to John, and when she moves to embrace him too quickly, John gets glassy-eyed. If John explores his trance state, he sees a scene where his mother hit him as a child. If they don't clear up this dreaming, John and Susan will stay stuck in a chronic pattern. At this stage they may start to fight. She accuses him of being cold and distant, and he accuses her of being sexually frigid. In such a situation, until the dream material is cleared up, all the couples therapy in the world will not work.

One further note on working with traditional sex roles. I have seen hundreds of teenagers suffering from what I call the absent father syndrome, which goes something like this. The teenager gets in more and more trouble at school, with the law, or with drug or alcohol involvement. The teenager particularly provokes the father to the point that he must get involved. As soon as the father starts going to conferences or therapy, the teenager's behavior improves rapidly. As soon as the father backs off, the behavior predictably starts again.

When fathers come in for family therapy, they are often ready to quit after a few weeks because the teenager is getting better. I usually warn them it may be too soon, since we are just starting to work out the deeper issues. I often tell parents in private that if they quit therapy so soon, they should not be surprised if the disturbing behavior reappears. It is up to the whole family to change their structure so it works for everyone. If these changes aren't made, the family often comes back to therapy, sometimes upset that they didn't get a cure. Some parents ask for a pill for the child to fix the problem disturbing the family.

Often the teenager is doing for the family system what the parents can't do. The teenager may be saying "We are too disconnected as a unit, I am floating out here on my own more than I am ready for." Often I tell families that they have a choice—to spend time with a teenager in some enjoyable way, or to spend time bailing their teenager out of trouble. One way or another, teens will get the attention they need.[10]

The fathers I work with are living the best way they know, yet the economic pressure is so great that keeping up financially is all they can do. But the way they were taught to parent was so incomplete that life keeps screaming at them to develop. Their wives, or children, or both, are pushing them to be more available. Many of the men I work with just don't understand.

---

[10] For those interested in family issues and family therapy, look for my book *Transforming Family Life: A Process-Oriented Approach to Working With Families*, forthcoming in 1999.

They are playing the game according to the rules they were taught, but the game is not working. I feel sad when I hear a family talk about how hard they have worked to provide for their children, and one is a drug addict, the other has dropped out of school, and both have left home by running away. My heart goes out to people in these situations.

BEYOND MATERIALISTIC VALUES

At the core of these problems is an issue with the American dream. When we watch television, or read magazines, we see support for material values and an emphasis on gaining more material goods. It is true that our children and perhaps our partners need us to provide for them materially. But this is not all that we need from one another. To become whole people, we must nourish all parts of ourselves. In many families, material support is emphasized at the expense of love, quality contact, emotional expression, and spiritual life. The emotional, interpersonal, physical, intellectual, and spiritual needs of both the individual and the family unit must be addressed if the unit is to have healthy, fulfilling functioning. When we go overboard with our emphasis on the material, the disturbers in our families force us to look at other essential pieces of life, as we saw in the absent father example above.

TOUGH LOVE AND OTHER PROGRAMS FOR HEALING THE FAMILY

Several years ago the tough love concept became popular. This theory suggests toughness as a solution to disturbing behavior by children. Tough love encourages parents to provide clear consequences for inappropriate behavior, up to and including forcing children out of the home. Tough love focuses primarily on the child's or teenager's symptom without looking at the family unit and what part of the process the disturber is carrying. Another way to ask this question is: what systemic changes is the youth moving the family towards through their disturbing behavior?

Systems tend to maintain homeostatic positions. The disturber forces movement, and this movement can't just be threatened away. If what is missing in a system is toughness, and the youth is pushing this to happen, then tough love could be just the ticket. However, any programmed approach to family problems makes me nervous, since each situation is unique and calls for its own solution. For example, some children need a gentler approach, and tough love may force them into longer-term inappropriate behavior.

I studied structural family therapy and was very impressed by the short-term results of this work. However, I stopped using structural family therapy as my regular approach with families because it is also a programmed approach, with an ideal of family functioning in the background. Structural family therapy supports empowering the parental unit. In this approach, the main causes of family problems are that families are either too disconnected or over-involved. The therapist enters into the family and attempts to balance the family so that a disengaged family becomes more involved and an over-involved family becomes more disengaged. This approach did not have as many positive long-term results as I would have liked, and I began question it as a sole approach. The more I studied process-oriented psychology, the more I understood the problem.

Families are unique living organisms that have tremendous meaning in how they organize themselves. Imposing structure may be right for one family, but may completely miss the mark in another. Let's take, for example, a family where Stan, the fourteen-year-old, is getting into more and more trouble in school. A structural change might mean that Stan's father has been too distant and needs to start spending more time with Stan. By bringing the two closer, Stan may change. Another structural change might be that Stan's mom and dad need support for becoming a strong parental unit. There is no discipline because Stan can divide and conquer. In many families, this kind of structural support is much needed. However, in other families, this won't work. Some kind of deeper development is being called for in the whole family unit, and Stan is just pointing the way.

Let's say that Stan is always getting in trouble for being so non-conformist. His parents both came from authoritarian families and were never allowed to explore the parts of themselves that didn't conform. The parents now live out their non-conformist sides on an occasional Saturday night when they become extremely drunk at the local bar, but they have never consciously developed their non-conforming sides. To really become themselves in life, they need to do this. A family process like this will not change, no matter how many structural changes are made. Usually, unless this deeper level is addressed, Stan's behavior, as the identified problem, will just get worse.

Another possibility is that his behavior may improve temporarily due to the structural changes, but then either Stan will show more disturbing behavior down the road, or the disturbing pattern will show up in another child or in physical symptoms, accidents, or other channels of expression. A workable approach needs to address the process that is happening and emerging in each family in addition to structural issues. Going beyond the given forms of a culture into what is truly trying to happen in relationships is exciting work that leads to sustainable changes based on integration rather than repression and suppression. Working for integration includes valuing the existing family structures. These structures have been attempting to do the best job possible of helping the family function. Family changes, like changes in a town, can't be made without supporting the primary processes of the family, strengthening and supporting the family structure and values. This often adds stability and strength to the family.

Process work allows the system to keep growing by valuing all parts and working with them to discover a more wholesome lifestyle. In the above example, the family needed to be supported for its desire to fit in, to conform, and to be seen as a highly respectable and responsible family. However, in the non-conformity that Stan brought up were all kinds of interesting creativity, fun, and freedom that the parents had given up. By addressing all of these parts, the family thrives in a new way; they actually get a child who isn't in trouble as often, as well as having access to more parts of themselves as parents. As the work with this family continued, both parents began to develop in places that had been inhibited. The mother became freer to express her anger, while the father felt freer to play and have fun. Stan was finally appreciated for his refusal to give up his own way of doing things, and was also free to be himself in other ways that did not get him into trouble.

LIFESTYLE STRUCTURES

Variety is also the key in terms of lifestyle arrangements in couples. Traditional marriage works for many people, and we need tremendous amounts of support from our societies, and from churches and temples and our families, to maintain this. However, we can't force people to stay in traditional modes. For some people, divorce is right, while others prefer remaining single. Some couples need a more open marriage that allows room for involvement with other people. I have worked with couples in relationships that range from the traditional monogamous marriage through all kinds of permutations and combinations. The only thing that seems to work predictably for couples is finding out who they really are and following that. I have seen people get involved in open marriages where both have numerous partners or a second partner. This will be a disaster if the couple does this because their friends do it or because they intellectually believe in it but it is not where they really are. On the other hand, if this is a true expression of who they are, it can work beautifully. Traditional marriage is fantastic for many couples, yet I have seen it be so oppressive that people develop physical symptoms and die as the only way out of the oppression.

Learning to tailor our relationship structures to fit the personalities and the needs of the people involved can be quite a challenge. There is a great deal of societal pressure to be either traditional or nontraditional, depending on our environment. Being a therapist is a bit like being a sociologist. Through studying what comes through my office door, I see what different trends are present in society and what people are trying to do about certain core problems. Most relationships have a few basic problems that manifest in many different forms, and studying them can tell us a lot about how society is developing and failing to develop.

As therapists and people involved in relationships, we need to learn to see that our problems are both our individual problems and the consequences of living in a society that has certain biases, prejudices, and styles. We need to be able to process our problems on different levels, and to know which level we are working on. During some relationship struggles we are working on the individual level, at times on the relationship level, and sometimes on a social level. Sometimes the work is personal growth; sometimes it is couples growth, and sometimes the awareness of social issues and becoming a social activist is important. When all of these levels are addressed, there are no hidden realms that can undermine progress being made.

CHAPTER VII

DRUG AND ALCOHOL PROBLEMS

Working in a small town has shown me the limitations of traditional ways of treating addictions and given me the perfect opportunity to study the effectiveness of process-oriented methods of addiction work. Traditional approaches to addiction emphasize stopping use of the substance. Process work emphasizes saying "no" to the substance, but also emphasizes saying "yes" to the part of the personality accessed and supported by the use of the substance. Often addictions support parts of the personality society doesn't encourage. For example, in an age of increasing tension and frenetic living, all kinds of relaxing substances are popular, especially alcohol and marijuana. We as individuals have our own addictions to grow out of, but let's not forget that our society needs to change too, and that individual and societal change go hand in hand. Substances become addictive psychologically because they help people live parts of themselves that need expression. In substance abuse, people find temporary solutions to knock out some of the intense cultural conditioning that limits their freedom.

For example, there is intense cultural pressure to work more hours to make more money to consume more. Alcohol can open the door to down time and relaxation. Getting drunk or stoned or wired on speed can be like drugging the jail guard so that you can take the keys and escape for awhile, only to be caught and have to suffer the consequences of escaping. But if you are desperate enough to escape, you will do it any way you can, including substance addiction. In small towns, community norms can become prison-like; it is hard to hide much of what goes on in a small town, and not fitting in with the norms can be devastating. Many people resort to substances as a way to access the parts of themselves that are outside cultural norms.

The small towns where I have worked all have had severe substance abuse problems, with alcohol and amphetamines most frequently abused. Key factors in this high rate of drug use are the boredom of small town living, the stresses of the kinds of work present, and a social life that includes heavy drug and alcohol consumption. Due to their isolation and strict social norms, small towns are breeding grounds for drug problems. Small towns are usually isolated, creating a perfect environment for hiding an amphetamine manufacturing business.

Most therapists in small towns use two popular approaches to working with addictions, both of which have some success. The first is the Twelve-Step approach of Alcoholics Anonymous (AA) and Narcotics Anonymous (NA). The second is an educational approach that teaches about the legal, health, and life consequences of drug abuse and that emphasizes staying clean. The process-oriented approach offers a third alternative that can be combined with other approaches.

Process work shares a great deal with the twelve-step programs. Both use a tough love, no-nonsense approach to substance addiction—supporting the person and their process, but being tough and clear and straight about confronting the addiction. Both are clear that dangerous addictive behaviors need to stop. Both are aware of the excuses and deceptions addicts use to justify their addictions. Sponsors in twelve-step programs know because they have been through all the tricks and deceptions themselves. Process workers who have not been substance addicted learn through experience and training to pick up the addict's lack of honesty around addictions. Since information on the twelve-step and educational models is widely available elsewhere, I will focus on the process-oriented approach to working with addictions.

Process work differs from twelve-step programs in that its confrontation of the addictive behavior is combined with helping people work on whatever is fueling the addiction. For example, if someone has a serious depression in the background, just cutting out the substance could be dangerous. Process work simultaneously addresses the depression in the background and the need to stop using the substance.

Process work with addiction aims to help individuals to discover the deep need fueling the addiction and to develop more sustainable and positive ways to express their needs. To be successful, the new expression needs to be more satisfying than the addiction, without its consequences. I remember working with a man who had been a serious alcoholic for years. At one point we discovered that his drinking began when, at a relatively young age, he had a traumatic experience and stopped pursuing friendships. We worked through the incident, supported him in creating new friendships, and his drinking stopped instantly. In follow-up over the months, he didn't begin drinking again. Alcohol was a dangerous substitute for the interpersonal contact he needed, so real friendship replaced his need for alcohol. The underlying need and the substance that is abused can be separated. While the substance is harmful, the need is often important and useful to the person's development. In this case, the background issue was his need for human contact.

Many approaches to drug treatment have a goal of eliminating use. In order to eliminate substance abuse over time, deeper underlying needs must be discovered, and the client must develop more effective ways to address these needs than those provided by the substance. The person must address the substance and the deeper underlying process, with an emphasis placed on the individual's need for support for certain parts of his or her personality. In the example of the man who needed friends, he sought out treatment when his drinking began to seriously affect his health. It was important to tell him to stop drinking, since drinking was killing him. However, this was only done in combination with building a new pathway of support to replace the role alcohol had played. Focusing on the underlying needs is the key to eliminating substance abuse over time, whether the emphasis of the treatment approach is educational, spiritual, or peer pressure.

BEYOND THE DISEASE MODEL

A major breakthrough in addiction work came when addictions stopped being identified as a moral deficiency and started to be addressed as diseases. This reduced the stigma of treatment. Along with the benefits of the disease model come some disadvantages. One of the limitations of the disease model is its emphasis on the fact that the person is ill. While this is a step away from thinking that the person is evil, as in the morality model, the emphasis is still on what is wrong with the person. This focus can build resistance in a person and make her feel even more out of personal control. The advantage to the process model is that it supports the wisdom of the person through stating that the addiction is trying to support a valuable part of the person. The problem is that the addiction supports the part in a way that makes the whole person sick. The end is the right end, but the means are a problem.

People tend to get excited about this model, and about discovering ways to get more of what they want without the negative effects of the substance. They focus not only on giving up the substance, but on getting more of what they need. This transition is not easy. Our example of the man who turned around his long-term alcohol problem so quickly can paint an unrealistic picture. For many people, giving up a substance is an incredible struggle, even with inpatient treatment, AA, and process work. Process work is not the magic answer; it just adds a powerful tool to work with addiction problems.

The personal meaning of an addiction varies. I have worked with several people who relate to marijuana or alcohol as their mother. They say things like, "I feel like the mother I never had is soothing me." In such cases it is important to focus on the issue of mothering and relaxation, discovering why the mothering didn't occur, how the person could get mothered now, and how they could mother themselves. People tend to respond well to this approach, in which the therapist works together with the person to help her learn how to care for herself without drinking or smoking, and to learn what stops her from being able to get what she needs. In many cases, this approach is effective because it is the path of least resistance. Instead of fighting the strength of an addiction through telling the person to stop and thus becoming an additional source of stress, the therapist supports the wisdom of the organism and helps people find healthier ways to get their needs met.

It is important to be able to distinguish the addictive process from the addiction itself, so that the underlying need is identified and supported. One way to discover the addictive process is to suggest that the person act as if they were on the substance. Most people can to some degree quickly access the state and start feeling and acting like they are on the drug. This is the beginning of awareness that drugs are not only substances but also states of consciousness that can be accessed without drugs. Once a person is in this state, the therapist and client together can identify what the substance does for the person, and then can work together to find other ways for the person to get the same effect.

Separating Underlying Needs From Substance Abuse

Let's look more closely at what might lie beneath an addictive process. I recently worked with someone I'll call Paul on his cigarette addiction. Since smoking gave him a minute to breathe and detach from his usual frantic state, picking up this detachment and supporting it was our task. While relaxation itself is important and healthful, cigarette smoking accesses relaxation in a deadly way. The therapist's task is to help separate the two. We knew that the only way Paul would stop smoking over time was if his new ways of relaxing were more effective and exciting than smoking. If Paul could learn to truly take time for himself, to detach and relax not just with a cigarette but as an ongoing part of life, then his cigarette use should fall away.

One of the most important parts of working on addictions is to help the person with the addiction access the state they are trying to reach. A word of caution is important here. Therapists need to be especially clear, when accessing a state of consciousness that the addiction supported, that they are in no way recommending that the person use the substance. The person's job is to learn to consciously access those parts of themselves that the substance gave them access to. Having this kind of access lessens the chances of the person's returning to the addiction. This approach helps the person get to the root of what was behind the addiction. The work must go far enough to give the person access to the state of consciousness in a deeper, more easily accessible, and more powerful way than the substance. It is important to give the person a physical way to remember that will anchor this experience of successful accessing, without the substance. For one person, it may be putting their head back, and for another, moving their arms slowly. The easiest way to find an anchor is to ask the person how they will remember the state they accessed, and watch what their body does. They will show you how they access this state, and the therapist needs to help them remember that whenever they need to go to this place, they can use their anchor rather than the substance. This approach of accessing the state works better with someone who is in the middle of abusing, or who has been away from substance use for at least a few months. There is a risk that a client who has just quit using, and who was repressing any feelings that the substance might access, might awaken a hunger for the substance. However, I have done this with hundreds of clients at various stages of using and recovery, and have never had this experience. Here are some examples of people who were able to use this approach to help them stop using.

When Paul smoked, he would look off into the distance and his jaw would drop. Over time, he learned to look out into the distance and relax his jaw in a certain way to access his state of relaxation without needing a cigarette. Discovering how to relax his jaw provided him a safe and effective way to get the relaxation he needed. Addictive substances are by definition harmful, and they also do an incomplete job of accessing the state. The substance gives a brief experience of what the person needs, but the need is met only momentarily. For example, while Paul was smoking, he also had physical symptoms of a tight jaw and grinding of the teeth. Learning to complete the relaxation state that smoking was attempting to reach also relieved him of his physical symptoms. His access to the relaxed state without smoking was over time more complete and more useful than the smoking had been. Once you integrate your addictive tendencies, your states of consciousness are accessible whenever you need them.

Let's look at another example. I remember working with a woman who hadn't smoked marijuana for quite a while and had recently started again after some very painful experiences. In her difficult times, she had not been able to relax and nurture herself much. When she smoked marijuana, she was able to access the relaxed state she needed for her healing. The only problem was that the marijuana was having other effects she didn't want, so she wanted to access the state she desperately needed without using a drug.

I asked her to just sit like she sits when she is really stoned, and we exaggerated that sitting position. Soon she started feeling like she had smoked a lot of marijuana, except that she could still think clearly, which wasn't the case when she really smoked marijuana. This woman was able to learn to sit in a specific position and gain the relaxation she needed for healing without needing to smoke marijuana and therefore without the side effects that had been disturbing to her.

TOWARDS A NEW VISION OF SUBSTANCE USE AND ABUSE

Because parts of ourselves that we need are hidden in addictions, campaigns that encourage people to "just say no" are popular but not highly effective. Saying no is a start, but once we say no to a substance, we need to say yes to our development. Processing the states behind addiction is one of the ways to support this development. We can see a pattern for accessing important parts of ourselves if we look at certain shamanistic cultures. Many tribes that once used hallucinogens to access altered states switched at some point to using drumming or dancing. What is important is not the substance, but accessing the state the substance provides. In some other cultures, like the Huichol of Mexico, the substance itself is considered sacred, and the substance as well as the state it accesses are both valued. In situations where a drug is used as part of an organized religion, it is taken with so much consciousness that addiction doesn't seem to be a problem. This is a much more complicated view of drug use than we are used to in this culture. More on this topic can be found in the books of Dr. Andrew Weil, who has written extensively about how the use of drugs for altered states of consciousness, in the right ceremonial context, might not be addictive.

In Oregon, the attorney general did not make a distinction between ritual and street drug use. In a case that went to the United States Supreme Court, he fought against Native Americans' rights to legally use peyote in ceremonies. In the atmosphere of terror that now exists around drugs, it is hard for us to imagine any spiritual benefits to drug use. But for many cultures, drugs have provided a way to step out of ordinary reality and connect with something greater as a source of wisdom, guidance, and inspiration for both one's own life path and the community. Visions gained through drugs might be the source of rituals or dance or personal wisdom or power. They might also lead to visions of healing for self or as a shaman to heal others.

Another example of positive results from drug use is the medical benefit of marijuana to relieve pain in cancer patients. I hope that as a culture we can keep an open mind so that we can work on addictions that are harmful, and focus less on those that aren't. For example, cigarette smoking kills hundreds of thousands of people each year, yet we send out the army to destroy marijuana crops while we subsidize tobacco growers. I am not saying marijuana is fine—I think there are more effective ways of accessing these states of consciousness that don't require drug use. However, if we have limited resources to address these problems as a culture, it makes sense to work to reduce alcohol and cigarette addiction, the causes of great damage, and to spend fewer of our resources fighting against peyote and marijuana, substances that some people find useful and some harmful. In my town, alcohol and cigarettes are the most dangerous drugs and most widely used, and crank, an amphetamine, is the other most dangerous and widely used drug. Treatment that offers people the opportunity to process their states is far more effective in eliminating substance abuse than all the police we can hire and prisons we can build.

CULTURAL IMPLICATIONS

Our culture tends to place responsibility for addiction on the individual and to ignore our collective responsibility both in creating and failing to address the underlying causes of addictions. For example, in small towns, in addition to tobacco and alcohol abuse, amphetamines are the drug of choice. Crank or speed, as the drugs are called on the street, represents the other side of small town living. Small towns have a slow pace of life, while speed gives people the feeling that everything is moving incredibly fast. People who use speed report that it accesses feelings of power, energy, sexual prowess, and wildness. In small towns, the limits and boundaries feel safe and confined. Speed gives certain people feelings of having infinite energy and being limitless. The states of speediness, limitlessness and power are all valuable and important balances to our ordinary states of consciousness. However, the old saying is true—speed kills. Its side effects are devastating.

The tendency toward wild states accessed through speed provides a necessary balance to small town life, but these states are deadly unless they are accessible through other means. Drug use balances our cultural one-sidedness, but we must find more productive ways of discovering all of ourselves. If those of us who live in small towns could consciously bring in wild, speedier, thrilling sides to life, if we were more open and experiential with life, not with drugs, we could help eliminate drug use. In my own small town, someone once tried to introduce basic yoga stretching into the schools—an idea that beats relaxing through drugs. There was such uproar from the community that the school district had to stop teaching the yoga stretches, which the community perceived as an Eastern cult religion.

In small towns we often think we can keep things safe and narrow, but forbidden experiences come out through drug use. In many small towns, people seek excitement through playing chicken in their cars—they get drunk and drive head-on at each other to see who chickens out and gets out of the way first. Many people don't chicken out and end up dying. Our collective challenge is to pick up this excitement consciously and live more exciting lives—at work, at play, with our families, in our relationships, intellectually, and spiritually. This is a big challenge for all of us who see that drug and alcohol use is partially an attempt to access parts of ourselves we need for our development.

Another example of the cultural implications of drug use is heroin. Historically, heroin is a drug used primarily in more impoverished areas, although its use has now spread through all economic levels. Heroin often makes people feel above it all, proud and whole. It helps them leave behind feeling trapped in the pain of their existence. These are important feelings to have, especially for those of us who feel trapped in a poverty-level existence. Like speed, heroin has terrible side effects. If we as a culture just say no to heroin, we avoid our responsibility for societal change. Let's take away the heroin, but let's also work to eliminate poverty. This approach is not very popular these days, but it is vital. Some addictions cannot be solved by individual work alone—the whole society must change.

LEGAL DRUG USE

Our technologically based culture offers us many advantages, but it also involves less and less human contact. As more of us adopt a less humane pace of life, drugs and alcohol substitute for human relationship and relaxation. This is not only true of illegal drugs. Prozac and other mind-altering drugs are dispensed by physicians like antibiotics used to be. These drugs give many people the support they need to function well. However, as a society, we must examine the down side of using legal and illegal, prescription and street substances as an attempt to fulfill deep human needs.

Our culture gives a huge double message—don't use drugs, but do use legal drugs. Don't use drugs and alcohol, but do be able to keep yourself running like a machine. Modern medicine in many ways supports the view that bodies are machines to be fixed with drugs and technology. Some doctors have forgotten the importance of the whole relationship between patient and doctor, which is exacerbated by the modern insurance system's pressure on physicians to see large numbers of people in a short time. The deeper needs of the human soul are rarely addressed in the doctor's office. Even prominent physicians are speaking out about the dehumanizing of the medical profession, which is becoming part of an economic system and culture that pressure people towards greater performance. In this view, getting well is rarely a matter of the soul, but of getting back to work.

Insurance companies instruct mental health providers that the purpose of health insurance is not to help people grow, but to get them back to a previous level of functioning. In this cultural reality, it is hard to stop addictions because they are in part a reaction to, and means of survival within, a mechanistic economic system and lifestyle. Process work can help people develop an awareness of the cultural pressures impacting them. This gives the individual more choice and support to develop an approach that works for them, even if that approach differs from the culturally approved way of being.

When I first started studying addictions, I felt tremendously relieved because I didn't seem to have any. I drink only an occasional beer, don't use drugs, and don't smoke, so I thought I didn't have any addictions. Then I began to look at addictions not only as substances, but also as behaviors, and I found several behaviors to which I am addicted. I was addicted to anger, which I was so invested in keeping that it cost me relationships. Much of this addiction came out of specific approaches to confrontation work I had studied. I got such a rush from fighting that it was hard to give it up. I needed to find a way to enjoy my rushes in a way that wouldn't destroy my relationships. Since I have worked on this behavioral addiction, I rarely have fights in my intimate relationships, and when I do they tend to resolve quickly.

The discovery of behavioral addictions has changed my views of addiction. Almost everyone I know is addicted to something, and therefore not totally free. One person is addicted to money, another to work, another to going to doctors, and another to shopping. I work with people who are addicted to crisis—they just have to find a crisis to be involved in, either their own or someone else's. No matter how exhausted they are or how much they have suffered, they are on to the next crisis.

Some people are addicted to certain kinds of relationships. I am reminded of one woman who found men who made love to her and then abandoned her. She would interview men, check them out in depth, and feel sure that she had finally found someone different. Then the pattern repeated, and she felt crushed. Working on this addiction was serious business, and this is a pattern I have seen in many clients. Another common behavioral addiction is to shopping with credit cards. Often in the background of this type of addiction is hopelessness around being loved and nurtured, and this background need must be explored.

Cultures have their addictions as well. In the United States our relationship to oil is certainly addictive—we ended up in a dangerous situation with Iraq over it. The anti-war cry became no blood for oil, but like heroin addicts who take terrible risks to get money to feed their habit, we as a culture feel we must spill blood to keep oil flowing through the veins of our economy.

Once we admit we are all addicts, we can have more compassion for those suffering from any addiction, because we are all in the same boat. Culturally based solutions, as well as therapeutic interventions, are needed. I am a strong believer that for most people repeated drug use is not a healthy thing, and needs to be eliminated, but the wisdom of the organism must be respected in terms of what it is trying to accomplish through using. This is true with even the most dangerous drugs, such as angel dust, or PCP, which has serious psychological side effects.

I remember working with a teenager who was having angel-dust flashbacks in which he was terrified by great streaks of lightning all around him. In another culture, his experience might have been considered a vision of power to be painted on his drum or ceremonial garb. Perhaps the medicine woman would have told him that he had a gift of working with the forces of nature, maybe to be a rainmaker. In this culture there is no context for understanding these experiences. Part of therapy with this young man included creating a context for his visual experiences. He related to the concept of being a visionary. This teenager was like many people who have amazing revelations about life through altered states, but he lacked a guide to help him make sense of and integrate what he was discovering.

Many people who have strong altered-state experiences don't see a therapist, or if they do, finding a therapist who knows how to work with altered states is rare. In the novel *Dreamspeaker*, a teenage boy is in serious trouble and keeps getting locked up. Finally he breaks out of an institution and ends up deep in the woods where he finds an old medicine man. When the boy finally tells the medicine man about the visions that haunt him and lead him into trouble, the medicine man says, "Yes, it is true what you are experiencing." This simple act of confirming the power and reality of the altered state made a huge difference in the boy's life.

The value of affirming an experience is often true with people experiencing psychotic states, but most traditional approaches attempt to convince people that these states are not real. In *City Shadows*, Mindell demonstrates the value of acknowledging that for the person, what is happening is very real. One of the greatest dangers I see in drug taking is that the right people aren't present to give meaning to the experience. Therapists need to learn more about helping people integrate and understand their altered states. We as therapists must lead the way in changing our cultural attitude toward addictions.

One cultural change that would be helpful is learning to support creativity. In *Witness to the Fire: Creativity and the Veil of Addiction*, Jungian analyst Linda Leonard writes about the clear lines between addiction and creativity. She talks about two powerful forces that fuel drug addiction: the demon lover, the part of addiction that lures people into more and more unhealthy states of being, and the creative demon, the spirit of creativity, that is also present in the individual.

While Leonard finds the twelve-step programs of Alcoholics Anonymous and Narcotics Anonymous useful for stopping the effects of the demon lover, she also sees a need for insight-oriented approaches such as Jungian analysis to help the creative power of the individual emerge in a way that is not tied to the substance. Both Mindell and Leonard believe that substance abuse is not only a disease, but potential creativity that could offer people relief and hope from feeling so awful about themselves. These feelings of guilt and shame are also addressed through the twelve-step programs, and these programs help people feel that addiction can be turned into a spiritual journey.

Process work and Leonard's Jungian approach help the individual process the specifics of their own creativity that have previously been accessed and supported by substance abuse. In small towns, the whole issue of boredom and its relationship to substance abuse needs to be addressed not only by therapists, but also by the whole community. Practical solutions are particularly crucial in small towns where there is often not a lot to do with one's free time. The awful toll drinking and driving takes, particularly on teenagers, is another reason to find solutions to the drug and alcohol crises.

Some practical solutions are already happening in many places around the country. My community is on the move in dealing with this problem. The schools have an excellent drug and alcohol counselor and peer support groups. Parents have organized successful non-alcohol parties for occasions such as graduation. More places in the community could host excellent non-alcohol dances, particularly off school grounds, which would make them more attractive. More recreation areas are needed to offer games like pool, supervised indoor hockey or soccer, basketball, and possibly computer use. In many small towns, there is a lot of support for teenage involvement in agriculture, forestry projects, raising animals, and other positive activities.

Martial arts can also be very beneficial. In the East the key to learning martial arts is developing discipline, concentration, self-respect, and often gentleness. Martial arts like Aikido, Tai Chi, and Chi Kung, which emphasize personal development as well as fighting ability, can be most useful. There are many activities besides substance abuse that can help teenagers live their excitement.

For teenagers, there is an additional problem in the background. Education has swung back to focus on basic reading, writing, and mathematics. This focus is important, since students must be educated to make it in the world. On the other hand, this swing back to basics has pushed out the movement toward affective education, or learning about oneself as well as about the factual world, which is also essential to making it. When I lead groups to help teenagers deal with their troubles around growing up, students talk about everything from their feelings about school to how they have been abused by their families. When we hear what teenagers really have to say, it is easy to understand why they have trouble concentrating in school, and why they may use drugs and alcohol to deal with their feelings and difficulties.

School can't be turned into a therapeutic community, because students who understand their emotions but can't read are not going to be very successful in the world. On the other hand, one of the main lessons I have learned through working with groups and organizations is that if some time is devoted to working on feelings, efficiency greatly increases. If young people were given more time to deal with their inner lives and their life issues, thus looking after what is really on their minds, academic learning would become easier.

Another reason to value psychological education is that basic skills for relating to people, expressing feelings, coping with stress, and resolving conflict mean more to a career than almost anything else. I have worked with many adults and young people who lost their jobs because they didn't know how to approach a boss or supervisor when they were upset.

If school provided students with opportunities to access their inner lives, it could compete directly with addictive substances. Many of the people I know who have learned how to work deeply on their inner experiences have given up using drugs. Deep inner experiences have no side effects—they are also free and completely legal. In more traditional cultures men took their teenage boys and women their teenage girls and put them though a series of initiations into adulthood. The teenagers were recognized for their abilities, challenged, and reassured that they had the support of their elders. Compare this with modern initiations—a group of teenagers goes out to prove how much they can drink. I have seen teenagers who drank so much at one time they ended up in the hospital close to death. We need to create modern rituals to help people make transitions between life stages in a more positive way. Drug abuse asks those in small towns and us as a larger culture to make fundamental changes in the way we live our lives.

CHAPTER VIII

ORGANIZING AND FACILITATING TOWN MEETINGS

In the last chapters on suicide, relationship problems, and addictions, I talked also about the need for social change as well as personal change. In small towns, social change means working on issues that the town itself needs to address.

When tensions or issues reach a peak in a small town, a possible course of action is to call a town meeting. I use this term in the process-work sense: a town meeting is a special form of worldwork dedicated to working publicly on conflict. The town meeting is open to the entire community, as opposed to special formats where only the participants in a conflict come together. As an example of the town meeting format, we will look at town meetings on various issues in small towns.

The first town meeting I'd like to discuss was on the topic of gay and lesbian issues. This town meeting came to pass during a period of time when tension was building over a coming vote on an anti-gay rights ballot measure. A woman from a gay rights organization initiated our meeting process by asking me if I could assist in any way with the tension. This looked like a perfect format for a town meeting. I asked Drs. Arnold and Amy Mindell for help with a community meeting, and we then invited the Oregon Citizens Alliance, the group that had initiated the anti-gay rights initiative.

Mindell has written about working with this particular issue. He says, "People in lesbian, gay and bisexual relationships endure enormous social deprecation.... Simply having most of the world believe there is something wrong, sick, perverted, abnormal, maladjusted, evil, or infantile about you is a pressure difficult to combat. Sometimes you almost believe it yourself."[11] These dynamics between the mainstream and the lesbian, gay, and bisexual minority are important to keep in mind when addressing this issue, since they are sure to be operating in the background.

Another important piece of information for working with any marginalized group issue is that of rank. Rank is the "conscious or unconscious, social or personal ability or power arising from culture, community support, personal psychology, and or spiritual power. Whether you earned or inherit your rank, it organizes much of your communication behavior."[12]

The problem with rank is that the more we have the more we become blind to the pain of others. Here is a simple analogy. A group of people is sleeping high in the mountains where it is very cold, and there are not enough blankets for everyone. The person who owns the inn has a wood stove and a comforter; he is so warm that it is easy for him to forget that others are cold. Rank is similar. The more rank I have, the more potential I have to help others, but the more removed I may become from the experiences of those with less rank. The classic dilemma with power centers on this question: how do we use our rank and privilege to feel for, care for, and uplift others? The more common choice is to use our rank to turn our backs, close our hearts, and oppress those with less rank. Rank brings with it unconsciousness, so it is only by developing our awareness that we are able to move into using our rank in a more compassionate way. We see this dynamic in the United States when members of congress say that poverty and hunger are no longer problems while people are starving and living in unbelievable poverty. If you have enough wealth and insulation, this narrow perspective starts to look like your world. Unless we make an

---

[11] Arnold Mindell, *Sitting in the Fire*, p. 69.
[12] Op. cit., p. 42.

effort to look outside our narrow field of vision, we might think that poverty truly is nonexistent. This is what enables us to make and believe statements such as "poverty is not a problem."

In situations of tension, like the pre-election time in this small town, we need a deep understanding of rank and its influence on group interactions. In a situation such as this one, much of the increasing tension is caused by the mainstream group's lack of awareness about its rank. The leader needs to know how to get the mainstream side to own their rank, use it consciously, and understand the impact their rank has on others of less social status. An additional task for the facilitator is to assist the marginalized group in bringing out their hurt, anger, and wisdom to help wake up the world.

Much worldwork training in the United States has focused on racism. Time after time, African Americans have awakened the white mainstream to the agony of daily living in a racist culture. Sometimes this work seems like trying to chop through blocks of ice that protect the white community from seeing and feeling the real suffering of racism. Yet the power to speak from the pain and realness of these experiences continues to wake up the mainstream's consciousness and ability to make changes.

In the situation of gay rights issues in a small town, both groups presented themselves as having low rank. Clearly the gay and lesbian group is an oppressed, marginalized group nationwide, and this status is even more exaggerated in small towns. One of the first openly lesbian women I worked with in a small town was beaten by her lover's brother when he found out they were together. Gay bashing and other forms of intimidation are common. Living in the closet is terribly oppressive, but it is often a necessary survival tactic. Suffering comes not only from physical intimidation, but also from the constant psychological, political, and economic oppression.

The anti-gay rights group also presented themselves in many ways as an oppressed minority. They had been abused by the press, harassed in public, and hurt. However, this group had a much more mainstream position and therefore far more rank. They also had more mainstream tactics, such as using the Bible for support of their side. They represented themselves as standing for the family values of the mainstream.

Since most rank is unconscious, the goal of the facilitator is to gently awaken both sides to their rank, and to encourage them to use it wisely. The facilitator tries to value all people and all sides and to bring awareness to the situation. Because the marginalized group has been hurt, often by the mainstream group they are facing in a town meeting, marginalized group members may have a tendency to seek revenge. This tendency is understandable, but simply hurting the mainstream back may increase the mainstream's tendency to be hurtful and unconsciousness.

An example of revenge is that a marginalized group, in a setting that supports them, might use the opportunity to hit back verbally at the mainstream group. This of course needs to happen, but sometimes the verbal attacks may get to the point where the mainstream people will literally walk out of the room. It may be emotionally satisfying for the marginalized group to burn up some fury in this way, and some mainstream groups will be able to listen and take it. Others will just close off and use this as further evidence to keep the marginalized group down. This revenge dynamic asks marginalized groups to do something that is possible and yet difficult—to see that at certain moments, they might also be oppressors as well as oppressed.

I have seen many different marginalized groups able to do this. I remember working in Israel with a group where an Arab man was addressing a group of Jewish Israelis. He talked of his hurt and his anger, and also said that he didn't want to go so far into these feelings that he couldn't maintain and build his relationships with Israeli Jews. He noticed the moments where he might be becoming oppressive, as well as expressing the unbelievable oppression his people experience. His ability and awareness in this complicated situation were truly awesome.[13]

Let's look at a few crucial points for those of us who might wish to facilitate community meetings. The first is to try to be aware of your rank, of the powers and privileges that you have, and then to utilize your power wisely. For example, it helps to state your rank as you are facilitating a meeting. If I am facilitating in Israel between Arabs and Jewish Israelis, I need to say that I am a man, a Jew, and an American, which gives me certain privileges in this particular setting. I have obvious economic rank in that I have flown around the world to facilitate. I am also from the United States, where there is less overt conflict and immediate danger on this issue. If I don't mention my rank due to these privileges, Jewish Israelis are likely to confront me about my ability to be more detached. Because I am Jewish, I have the privilege of whisking through security at the airport; I can travel freely and be treated well.

A special kind of rank comes with being a facilitator. After one of my workshops in Israel, a man from eastern Europe said that he must talk to me. Although he knew little about me aside from my position, he begged me to tell the world about his country's plight. The position of facilitator, of expert, brings power. The challenge is to use this power to help people grow and help the world change, rather than using the position to shove my individual views across.

Once aware of my privileges, can I try to spread this awareness of rank and privilege to others? This is the work of the facilitator. If I am not up for this, the chances of real transformation are greatly reduced, because my bias and putting others down will block rather than free the interaction that needs to happen. When people are aware of their rank and privilege, no matter what side of the issue they are on, they are less likely to be hurtful. To get people to come to a town meeting, I need to be congruent in my concern for all sides, and be able to give

---

[13] For those interested in deeper understanding of how to work with such situations, I suggest Mindell's *Sitting in the Fire.*

people a feeling that they will be treated well and with care even in the hottest situations.

In the martial arts, I learned very early that the person least likely to hurt me was someone aware of his or her strength, an advanced practitioner. The most likely person to hurt me was someone who was very powerful and didn't know how to use his or her power. One goal in a town meeting is to help everyone involved become aware of their various strengths and engage in as conscious a battle as possible.

The town meeting brings together all sides in a conflict plus anyone else who wants to come. There are a few keys to a good town meeting. The first is to try to get both sides to show up. In the case of this particular conflict, this was very difficult. I had to convince the Oregon Citizens Alliance that they would be protected and that we would keep the meeting fair and neutral. They took a risk and attended. Afterwards, one of their leaders said that it was the first time they had felt treated fairly in a public debate. I also had to encourage the gay and lesbian community to believe that dialogue would help, and that dialogue was just as useful as fighting back.

I believe in the town meeting process, and my enthusiasm encouraged others. I encouraged people to attend because I really believed things could get better. I had once facilitated a similar process in a large city. At that time, after hours of tension, the male leader of the gay community and the male leader of the fundamentalist group ended up hugging and telling each other steps they would take to stop hurting each other. This success was the basis for my confidence.

Once the sides agree to show up, the next step is to get a facilitator, which could be one person, two people, or a group. The facilitator makes sure that after one side speaks, the other side gets to speak. A good facilitator in a town meeting tries to direct the level of emotion to a level the group can handle.

She follows the group's ability to tolerate strong emotions as the meeting progresses. It is helpful to start the processing, after introductions, with inviting pre-arranged speakers to represent different polarities present. In his spring 1999 classes on facilitating town meetings, Mindell recommends bringing up speakers who represent more extreme positions present in the group. By doing this, we help to bring out the ghost roles, or the hidden positions, in the group process. The ghost roles are positions in a room held by individuals, or groups of individuals, that are present, but usually not recognized or spoken about. Part of the ghost role may be the strong opinions or feelings present but not represented.

For example, at a town meeting on racism, we asked people who were strong civil rights activists to speak along with the mayor and a neo-Nazi. All of these are potential ghost roles— the civil rights leader may not have felt free to speak in a mostly white group. The mayor and government and the police are often present at town meetings and sit quietly and watch what is happening. Overt racists are present in the town and the meeting, but often strike at the city in hidden ways.

The theory behind inviting someone like this to a town meeting is, first of all, that their presence will stimulate a great deal of discussion about racism. For several weeks after the meeting, people came up to me and told me they had been discussing the meeting and what occurred there. Racism had become a topic for people to discuss openly. The meeting was on the front page of the paper, on many television stations, and generated debate in the alternative newspapers.

The second part of the theory is that any group, no matter how extreme, is less dangerous to a town when they have their say in a public arena where they can be seen and related to. Most groups like this operate in the shadows of the night, and are less dangerous if they are out in the open. On some occasions, I have seen extremist leaders change on the spot from the intensity of the interchanges at a town meeting. Having someone present in no way implies any kind of approval or support. It simply means these people are in our town, let's see them, and have it out directly.

A third part of the theory is that people may then also work on this part of themselves. Several people told me that they hated the neo-Nazi so much that they were forded to look at where they themselves are a bit like him. Bringing someone so controversial is a strong move, meant to help shake the town out of its complacency towards the racism that is happening, not only from the extremist group, but in all of us who are part of the mainstream and not working enough on our racism.

By putting these speakers first, we invite them to be seen in the light of the day and also to be addressed and responded to. Later in the meeting, we broke up into small groups, and fifty people confronted the neo-Nazi.

Mindell also points out that, in a town meeting, facilitators need to remember that any issue is an umbrella for all the issues under it. When we work on racism, we will find that sexism, classism, anti-Semitism, or homophobia are all waiting to come forward. Within any topic is the whole world. One way to help the people in the meeting understand what is happening is for the facilitators to frame what is happening; for example, 'Now we are focusing on racism, and people are also raising issues of sexism" and how the two are related. The facilitators don't just let the dialogue go on, but put a frame around what is happening at any given moment. It is also helpful to frame what levels are being addressed in the meeting. An individual focusing on her own psychology or stories may be addressing the personal level. When two people or two groups get in a conflict or begin to interact, the relationship level is present. Other times people may address systemic concerns with the whole political and social system. Putting a frame around the level helps people understand what is happening, and understand that all levels are relevant and part of the larger issues being addressed.

Even if the facilitator is on one side or the other, a good facilitator tries to value both sides and values the flow of communication more than either side winning. While most polarized groups want to win, the facilitator views success as people communicating with each other. Another job of the facilitator is to hold down hot moments that come up by recognizing them and asking the group for consensus to focus on them. Hot moments that are skipped over tend to come back and also tend to lead to unnecessary escalation. A facilitator who can hold down hot spots can work with dangerous tensions safely. The good facilitator also creates a framework for tensions to emerge and be dealt with. A useful facilitator adds awareness to the field by commenting on what is happening, and on what may be coming next. These skills of valuing all sides, focusing on hot moments, reporting, and gaining consensus, are all skills that we can learn and practice in our relationships, our families, our work, and our world.[14]

When I lead workshops on facilitation, the steps for facilitating a group, from start to finish, begin with *sorting,* i.e., finding out what issues are present. Next, the facilitator needs to gain consensus from the group to focus on a certain topic. Consensus may also be required to agree on a style of processing, such as linear or free flowing. The next task is to bring out the different sides present on the issue. In a town meeting, this is often structured by first inviting people who represent the different sides; afterwards the rest of the people come in. The next job of the facilitator is to hold down the focus at the intense moments. Mindell says not to push, but to try up to three times to get the group to focus on an intense moment. The facilitator needs to keep this process of interaction going, making sure that all sides get to speak and be heard, and help the sides respond to each other. As the meeting approaches its end, it is important to spend some time focusing on where we as a group go from here. People need to feel a sense of continuity, and that the important work they have done together will go forward. It is vital for the facilitators to help summarize where the meeting went, where it didn't go, and what the next steps are. In addition, it is also important to appreciate everyone for coming,

---

[14] For more information on working with hot spots, see Mindell's *Sitting in the Fire*, pp. 80-81.

knowing that many people took risks in opening themselves up to the reality of what is happening in their town. A town meeting may also expose people to more conflict and emotion than they are used to experiencing.

One of the most amazing things that happened at this meeting—which consisted of the Oregon Citizens Alliance, the local gay and lesbian community, and the local community—was that people from the Oregon Citizens Alliance began to show who they were personally. We began to see the real person under all of their opposition to gays and lesbians. Many people talked about the pain in their lives. The Mindells are masters at helping people get to a more human level where it is not just issue against issue, but person to person. On this human level, we are all more alike than we often want to admit when polarized. Both sides could relate to pain, since both sides had been through incredibly hurtful situations. It became clear during the meeting that when we are working with a person or group that has a great deal of prejudice, it is not enough to confront them. People move past their prejudices only after the hurt their bitterness is built upon is understood.

After the town meeting, the Oregon Citizens Alliance's ballot measure won. But winning a political battle, in my view, is not a solution, since it is a one-sided triumph that leads to revenge and an ongoing cycle where nobody wins for long. The idea that "might makes right" leads to oppression. What is more important is that pathways for dialogue are opened, and that communication shifts from cold stares to open discussion.

A couple of years have passed since the meeting took place. This particular small town still isn't a center for openness to gays and lesbians, but there hasn't been any overt violence, that I am aware of, directed at gays and lesbians, as there was in other small towns. The tensions are still present, yet many gays and lesbians live in this town and feel good about it. One of the changes in public opinion after the town meeting may have been a decrease in harassment about sexual identity, although there was no public statement in support of gay and lesbian rights. While many still spew forth hatred, many others learned and opened up, and the town became more diverse in its perspective. There is still more to discuss on this issue. In our town, as in most others, it is an ongoing struggle, but we have now created a pattern—if tensions build, we can enter dialogue around them.

This basic pattern about the hurt that lies behind prejudice is apparent in many settings. Recently I came upon a scene on the street where there was an encounter between a group of very alternative people dressed in the hippie style and a man carrying a sign trying to close down one of the biggest hippie celebrations on the West Coast. The exchange got more and more heated. I asked the man trying to close down the celebration why he was talking in such a derogatory, prejudiced way to the group of hippies. He was very hostile at first, but then I also told the group of hippies that he was courageous for speaking his mind to such a large hostile group and deserved respect. As I won some of his trust, he began to tell us what was behind his prejudice. He began to talk of painful issues in his personal and family life, including the death of one of his children. These personal stories were the basis for his political stance. His sharing temporarily helped with the crisis, since people could relate to his story.

Similarly, in a gay and lesbian group process I facilitated, the turning point came when one of the anti-gay leaders talked about how he had struggled and tried to repress his own attractions to men so that he wouldn't hurt his family. This amazing disclosure moved the whole scene to a more human level. In extreme polarization and even war, the other side ceases to be human, and then it becomes possible to inflict the worst possible suffering on that side. The facilitator's job is to keep the tensions coming to the foreground, but also to keep people seeing each other's humanity. The differences must be worked on, but we also need to remember that we are all people with similarities. In moments of real clarity in a group process like this, one side knows who they are, but can also see aspects of the other side in themselves.

My own experience teaches me that I can only oppress others in areas where I myself am unconscious, often due to the amount of trauma I have had. Where I am hurt, and where I see others hurt, it is very easy at times to hurt others. It is only by waking up to my own hurt that I can become sensitive to others. The reverse is also sometimes true—that I can only become aware of my own hurt through studying and learning about the hurt of others. For example, I, as a Jewish person, have learned a great deal about the suffering that Jews have gone through by watching African Americans work on similar issues. Their courage to confront and own their own pain has given me the courage to explore my own.

If I explore and know my own pain, there is less chance that I will unconsciously hurt people in other marginalized groups. Through this development of awareness, we can build a world where we can appreciate each other's differences and learn to live together with these differences, knowing that we are all essential parts of the whole. The world worker knows that the amount of oppression and hatred in the world is so great that the place to start addressing it is wherever one encounters it.

Worldwork needs to happen at every moment. It needs to happen when someone makes a racist comment, when there is a fight in the street. In the private therapy office, it means that I can't let it go when someone speaks of hating homosexuals, makes an anti-Semitic comment, or shares their racist fantasies. Worldwork means calling a town meeting when tensions erupt in the streets, at the school, or at the grocery store. The world worker doesn't wait for a riot or a murder, but tries to intervene where she can.

The first basic step is to notice when something painful, important, or of social significance has happened. If the issue is important to others, the next step is to call a town meeting. Remember to be prepared for the difficulty of getting both sides to show up, since they have been hurt in public, distrust the media, and have other hesitancies. If you are the meeting organizer and/or facilitator, remember the personal rank you have and the rank this position gives you. Establish your rank and then use it to give everyone a sense that what will happen will be emotionally genuine, and that you will do anything you can to see that all are treated fairly.

When it is time to facilitate, if you are part of the facilitating team, remember to first work on your own issues relative to the topic so that you can keep your awareness. Try to make sure all sides get "airtime," which helps people feel that they are being treated fairly. Grab hot spots at their earliest emergence. Hold onto the heated spot and try to go deeply into the conflicts presented, since unaddressed hot spots can turn into wildfires. After all sides interact, make sure to set up committees or discussion groups so that the process doesn't go underground again. Remember to thank everyone for coming and to acknowledge that facing the real world and real human interactions in a group takes courage. Remember that the effects of these meetings are not always readily apparent, and may take weeks or months to show up. Don't be too discouraged; over time, town meetings are a sure way to facilitate community growth and change.

Chapter IX

Racism and Small Town Living

One of the ugliest sides of small town living is racism. Overt racism may be less obvious because so few people of color live in the many small towns in the northern part of the United States. However, the small number of people of color in these towns often indicates the amount of racism present. Mindell defines racism as "the intentional or unintentional and unconscious use of the mainstream race's political power against another race with less social power."[15] He goes on to say that "racism refers to the use of mainstream rank against people who don't have enough social power to defend themselves.... Facilitators—especially those from the mainstream—must realize that racism is economic, institutional, national, personal, interpersonal, and psychological."[16]

The state of Oregon, where I live, has a long history of white hate groups such as the Ku Klux Klan keeping small towns white. But racism is not limited to hate groups; it appears in all of us in the white majority. I have asked many people of color why they don't live in rural Oregon, and they say that if you value your health, you don't live in small towns in this area. Nationwide, there are small towns where people of different races live in harmony, and other small towns where church burning and other acts of hatred are common. There are small towns where the residents are primarily, or exclusively, people

---

[15] Arnold Mindell, *Sitting in the Fire,* p. 151.
[16] Ibid.

of color. In one of the towns I worked in, the only African American family in town almost had their house burned down. When I met with the man of this household, who had stopped the people who tried to burn his house down, he said that this was nothing new. They had had many death threats, and his family home in the Midwest had been burned down. The small town people wanted them out at any cost in both places. We must take a serious look at how this kind of hatred can still be so prevalent, and what small towns can do about it.

A GANG OF WHITE YOUTH SHOWS THEIR HATRED

Nationwide, the previous physical majority of white people is shifting. In our area, there are growing numbers of people who are Hispanic. This is pushing the issue of racism to the foreground, and the forces of hate are rising. The most obvious sign of this hatred was reflected in a group of white high school boys forming a group to harass students of color. There were several severe fights provoked by the group of whites. Families of the students attacked feared for their children's safety. Gradually, the name-calling and physical confrontations grew more serious.

THE TOWN MOVES TO ACT

The first thing that happened was several citizen groups were formed to fight the growing racism. Specific plans to reduce racial tension included a march, information and education meetings, and specific community events such as a public celebration of Cinco de Mayo. Multiracial committees began to meet to support those who had been victims of discrimination. I contacted different civic leaders, and we organized a town meeting, which the Mindells facilitated.

The highlight of the meeting was when many people of color began to talk openly about what they had been through. There was a great deal of strong emotion. Some of the whites began to talk about their own racism. The dialogue went back and forth, with whites trying to understand the experiences that the people of color had repeatedly had. Many others expressed pain about discrimination. While other meetings had focused on solutions, this meeting was a time for the community to search its own soul. People listened in detail, and sometimes in shock, to the stories. One Hispanic police officer talked about the hatred he constantly faced. This town meeting provided a start for people to try to understand each other and a forum to talk about how to move forward. After the meeting, we formed a committee to keep looking into these feelings and incidents. People also organized to watch the home that had been threatened with burning.

One of the most important ways to work on racism is to keep it at the forefront of people's minds. It is so easy to retreat to our homes, and to forget that this is a country in the midst of enormous racial difficulties. Town meetings are important ways for small towns to begin generating awareness about racism and to start doing something about it. The lack of information many of us who live in small towns have about racism helps perpetuate it. We need to know what is happening and then take action.

INDIVIDUAL SOLUTIONS TO DISCRIMINATION

As people begin to understand racism, they often wonder what they can do about it. Mindell outlines the work perfectly in *Sitting in the Fire*, saying that, "the only way a mainstream person can avoid being racist is to be awake all the time." Black Nationalist leader Kuame Ture said it similarly in a 1990 interview with David Basrsamian: "The only way you can say you are not racist is if you are struggling against racism in every aspect of life!"[17]

We can all clean out our own racism closets. A first step is to learn about our own subtle and overt racist thoughts and actions. It is also important to understand the kinds of rank and power that each of us carry, and to learn to use this rank and

---

[17] Arnold Mindell, *Sitting in the Fire,* p. 153.

power consciously. In issues of race, having white skin in this culture is a source of rank. Since it is easier for whites to obtain an education and make a living, these, as well as skin color, are sources of rank. For people of color, sources of rank often revolve around the spiritual power that comes from learning to cope with tremendous oppression. Spiritual rank is often present in marginalized groups as part of the spiritual traditions involved in their culture. For example, many African Americans are connected to spirituality through their involvement in Christian churches, the Black Muslims, or spirituality related to their African roots. Many people relate to several of these roads of spirituality.

One important way to work on racism is to think in your mind what specific prejudices you place on other people, and then learn to take back these projections. If I think Jewish people are too materialistic, I must ask where I am out of contact with my own materialism and love of money. Much of discrimination is based on projecting the parts of ourselves we don't identify with others. Since we can't stand these parts of ourselves, we can't tolerate these traits in others. People need to be educated to understand that hating others is not only destructive to the other, but to oneself. We are the other. We dream about people of all colors, genders, sexual orientations, and religions. These are parts of ourselves. Hating others means that we hate and marginalize those parts of ourselves we associate with the person we are prejudiced against. If I am homophobic, not only do I oppress others, but I oppress certain thoughts, feelings, movements, and other forms of expression in myself. Many heterosexual men are so homophobic that they marginalize all of their own softness, which helps destroy their relationships with their partners and families. If I am racist, then I am against all the parts of myself that I associate with the other.

The first step is to work to integrate these parts rather than just projecting them onto the other. The next step is to study ourselves and weed out the prejudice that runs through us every day. People learn to be racist from their families, their friends, and their culture. If a person watches television at night, he might easily become terrified of all black men, since so many police dramas show white police arresting violent men of color. The media help perpetuate degrading stereotypes. It is important to notice and challenge the racist assumptions that are perpetuated all around us.

In addition, it is vital to study and confront our own thoughts. If you are a white person walking down the street and a person of color approaches you, study your mind and find out if there is any prejudice in your response. All people who do not belong to a marginalized group have some elements of prejudice because the prejudiced attitudes pervade our unexamined assumptions about life and need to be weeded out.

A third step in inner work is to try to understand where the prejudice came from. I remember working with a man who made racist jokes and showed other forms of prejudice in the first session. When he made a joke about Jews, I told him how offended I was as a Jewish person. He couldn't understand why I was upset. As we worked on this, he told me that he had come from a family that had been racist for generations. He wasn't even aware of how his racism poured out of him. Family backgrounds are a huge source of racism, while some racism comes from being part of the culture, watching television, and hearing racist comments at school.

I remember one man who, as a child, had a scary experience with a person of color; as an adult, he unconsciously held this against every person of color. It is important to clean out racism on a personal level, right down to its root. Many people need to be challenged to break generations of racist thinking. Others need to clean up a one-time experience that became generalized. All of us need to work on the racism we pick up from living in this culture.

SOCIAL ACTION ON RACISM

Mindell clearly outlines the need for social action beyond changing oneself. He says, "In my view, if you only change yourself and take that to be more important than anything else you could do, you make a political statement to the effect that you are independent of other people, spirits, animals, and the environment. You may say: I love everybody. Let them develop on their own. But I say: Your laissez-faire attitude is not tolerance. It is a form of self-indulgence. It is Eurocentric philosophy, Eastern passivity, and plain middle class laziness. You appear to treat the world around you with compassion, but actually you erode your relationships with it by avoiding the discomforts of interaction."[18] He goes on to say that, "One virulent source of racism—the mainstream's alleged impotence to change the world—would disappear tomorrow if we realized that addressing conflicts and creating good relationships are keys to a meaningful life. Until you as a mainstream person address conflicts of rank and race, you must answer the question, 'Who is racist?' with, 'I am.'[19]

Social action begins in the moment, confronting and addressing racism in yourself, your family, your workplace, and wherever you come across it. There is plenty of opportunity for this kind of social action in one's backyard. There are also opportunities to address issues of race in local, national, and international issues. These days racism is often presented as an economic issue, or in other such terms, which ignore the underlying personal hatred. In major newspapers, it is common to find columnists saying that affirmative action and other such programs are no longer relevant since racism is a thing of the past. To confront these myths and lies, people can write letters to their papers, go to city and county meetings, and press their

---

[18] Arnold Mindell, *Sitting in the Fire,* p. 156.
[19] Ibid.

government representatives to not pass legislation that is racism wrapped in pretty paper that make it look less harmful.

Schools are a great place to call meetings on racism. Two years ago a local school asked me if I would meet with the parents of a class that was having enormous problems. Almost half of the children had asked to be transferred to other classes. When we met, I noticed that people of all colors were present. I asked if discrimination might be part of the problem the children were having. A white couple next to me said, "Of course not," and then people of color began to talk about what their children had gone through. The white couple was at first stunned, and then began to cry. They had never even imagined that such things could go on in a progressive school. Not talking about racism makes it even more painful and deadly. Educational forums and multicultural events are important. It may also be very helpful to call a town meeting, as described in the previous chapter.

RACISM AND HEALTH

There is increasing research into why some racial groups experience a higher incidence of certain physical symptoms. Among African Americans, a great deal of focus has been given to high blood pressure. There have been major studies of the high levels of cervical cancer in Hispanic women. While most studies focus on health care accessibility and genetics, it is also important to look at racism as a cause of health problems. The pain and tension of discrimination are extremely stressful on the body. It is essential to design studies that show the effects of discrimination on blood pressure, cancer development, and similar issues.

For many people, finding a way to come to grips with discrimination can be a matter of life and death. Death threatens both in the form of outside physical threats from people, and from the inside, in the form of threats to health caused by pain and stress. Racism, and the stress of ill health, are everyone's problems. We all live in the same world.

In my small town, where people of color are few, our children attend mostly white schools. They miss the benefits of multicultural experience and are deprived of opportunities to learn about people who look different than they do. This leaves them unprepared for the rest of the world. In much of the world, and in more and more places in the United States, whites are minorities. Hiding out in small towns and acting as if this isn't true isn't working for anyone.

Small towns have beauty, fresh air, and other appealing aspects, and people of all colors need to have access to this beauty. One of the subtle forms of racism is that many people of color cannot afford to live outside big cities. Companies often pollute the most in areas that are economically deprived. Since people of color have much higher rates of poverty than whites in this culture, pollution impacts people of color to a much greater degree. We need to make sure that small towns are affordable for everyone.

However, until we address the racism so often present in small towns, it acts as another form of deadly pollution that makes it unsafe for people of color to live in many of these places. Those of us who are white need to own the advantages we have because of our skin color, and utilize these advantages to help those who are discriminated against. We need to help people in small towns become aware of their racism, and take down the walls that have unofficially forbidden people of color from living in, and enjoying, the benefits of small towns. The activism that we can learn in our small towns can then be applied to the other experiences we have on the state level, nationally, and internationally. Small towns have been perfect breeding grounds for racism, but they are also ideal training grounds for informed, aware social activists who can confront and eliminate racism.

PART TWO

DAILY LIVING AS THERAPY

CHAPTER X

LIFE AS THERAPY

FOSTERING EARTHY INDEPENDENCE

Thus far, we have been looking at serious problems and crisis situations in people's lives and exploring ways to address these difficulties. An additional beauty of process-oriented psychology is that people can benefit from it every day, not just in the therapist's office. Living in a small town has taught me to respect a practical attitude towards life and a sense of earthiness that I sometimes find missing in my city practice. This sense of practicality leads me to address the issue of how to build therapy into one's daily life. If therapy is to be effective and available at the grassroots level, people must be able to do as much self-care as possible. Otherwise, time and financial constraints severely limit how many people can get therapy.

I have learned a lot from small town people about the spirit of independence, about learning to fix everything from your broken car to your wounded psyche without professional help. This spirit of independence motivates me to write about what people can do to help themselves when there is no therapist around. Another motivation behind this second section is my desire to see the whole field I call holistic healing move beyond any specific groups and into the masses. Certain teachings are common to almost all of the approaches I have studied, and people can use these approaches to work on themselves without a therapist. There is also a common message that the current time period is a particularly important time for people to be working on themselves. Some approaches take the more negative view, saying that we are entering a time of great crisis on the earth and we had better be prepared. Others are more optimistic, saying that we are at a time of great potential growth and should make use of the available energy. All approaches agree that we have much to learn about living life fully, and people need tools to do this.

WHEN TO WORK WITH A THERAPIST, WHEN BY YOURSELF

The approaches that follow are not meant to be a substitute for therapy, but a supplement. There are some excellent indications for when one should not attempt to work alone without a therapist. I see many people who say they have been doing fine with much of their own personal work but don't feel comfortable working on a certain piece alone. It is too scary, intense, hard to access, or difficult to understand. Believing and trusting oneself is crucial to this work. For most of us, learning to trust ourselves in a culture that worships experts is a huge task in itself. It's important to get professional help and not work on something yourself if you feel you need help. Professional help is useful when you are stuck or under time pressure to make certain decisions in your life. Seeing a professional is important when what you are doing is not working. It is also important when you get into such deep material that it begins to interfere with your work, relationships, and health in ways that are not useful to you.

Professional help is particularly important for chronic relationship problems. While I include some material on how to work on relationship problems alone, this is a difficult job. Someone needs to keep the therapeutic role to work on any problem. In most relationship conflicts and difficulties, this is extremely difficult unless you have had a lot of training.

There are several other areas where it is difficult to make progress without the help of a therapist. These include drug and alcohol addiction, extreme states such as psychosis and spiritual emergencies resembling psychoses, and behavior that is dangerous to a person or those around the person, including feeling suicidal or homicidal, being involved in physically or sexually abusing someone else, and other extreme situations.

In addition, how a person uses professional help is individual and depends on a person's process at the time. Some people might see a therapist once in order to get the next piece to work on, and then return a year later. Other people come for a significant number of sessions to work through a specific issue or problem. Some people need a guide or support and come to therapy for years for this purpose. Some just need a map, and others take their compass and go off alone completely. Since people have different needs in regard to therapy, I don't believe in having a program that asks people to come four times a week, or limits therapy to a maximum number of sessions.

If a therapist can follow a person's process, the therapist will provide the necessary help without making the person overly dependent, and without sending them into deep waters without adequate support. It is a delicate balance. There is a strong preventative element to personal growth work, so that people doing this work regularly may not need to develop a relationship crisis, serious personal problem, or severe illness. Each day offers material that can be worked with, including dreams, body sensations, and relationship issues. As we work on ourselves, life begins to seem more meaningful, and we can learn to understand more the meaning of day-to-day occurrences in our lives.

Here's an example of how we can use therapeutic thinking and tools in everyday life. I was vacationing in Hawaii. One day I put my leg up on a stone wall surrounding a palm tree. Although I had not put any weight on the wall, it fell down. I was not seriously injured, but I cut my leg and hurt it enough that I felt I needed to work on what happened. After the bleeding stopped and I was comfortable, I began to work on the experience. A theme emerged about needing to balance how much I feel pushed in life, and how much I feel supported, both by others and myself. I had worked on this theme before, but this time I really got the message and worked it through. A whole series of mini-traumas I had been experiencing that week stopped. Normally, when we have an accident like this, we get some bandages and go on. However, I am convinced that what happens to us in life is meaningful. When I get a message this loud and clear, I don't want to miss it and I want to get all I can from the experience.

One possibility is that nature starts trying to get our attention with low-level signals, which tend to get more dramatic as time goes on. Nature reminds me of my friend's five-year-old. When she wants our attention, she starts quietly, and if she doesn't get it easily, each attempt becomes more dramatic. There is no blame here—sometimes we can't pay attention, and in inner work, it is difficult to be conscious of so much going on. Nature is our ally in that she gives us many chances to pick up important signals, in many different forms and at various levels of volume. In terms of my leg wound, I picked this message up at the level of mini-trauma. To get my attention next time may have taken a bigger trauma. When I described my experience to some different local people, they said I was very lucky. People who are cut by lava or coral in that area and then swim in the ocean there often get severe infections from the waters. I believe that the trauma didn't go further partially because I sat with the experience and worked with it over and over again, milking the message from it.

Another way to work on ourselves is to look at our dreams each morning. While many people don't have time to do this every day, dreamwork is very valuable when one has the time or when material seems especially significant. Also, the more people experience dreamwork with a therapist, and the more we work on ourselves alone, the faster we get at doing it, to the point that it takes only a few minutes. Often I can do a piece of work on myself in five to ten minutes. I recommend that therapists learn to do dreamwork for your own benefit, and so you can help your clients benefit from the richness of their dream life. Little pieces of work we do on ourselves while we have ten minutes between clients can be truly revitalizing. Working on your own dream life as a therapist keeps you aware of what you bring with you each day into the therapeutic setting. Clients can stir so many different responses in you that it is helpful to know what is in your conscious and dream world before they enter your everyday world.

LIFE AS GRIST FOR THE MILL

Part of the beauty of working on oneself is that all of life becomes an opportunity for growth. The only goal is to bring added consciousness to whatever is already happening and unfolding in our lives. Sometimes people learning this work swing to an extreme and want to process nonstop, working on their relationships until the middle of the night. There are great discussions about the meaning of each event in each day. Usually, this excitement is soon integrated and people stop driving each other crazy and start living more consciously.

Real life experiences can be tremendously therapeutic. In *Gestalt Therapy Integrated*, Irving Pollster said that one good relationship is worth months of therapy. Therapy is not a replacement for living. When therapy and life are going well, they tend to resemble each other a great deal.

Therapy offers support to get more data and processing so that life's experiences become even more meaningful, pleasurable, and valued. Eventually one gets to a certain place where all of life becomes one's teacher. Experiences are faced as opportunities for growth, and we can learn much about others and ourselves from such daily life occurrences as a trip to the grocery. We do these ordinary tasks, but we do them with consciousness instead of on automatic pilot. Sometimes automatic pilot is necessary, but it is nice to also have the choice to do life's daily tasks in a conscious fashion.

Part of the problem with conscious awareness is the pace of modern life. When I am on vacation, my level of awareness of myself goes way up. It is hard to maintain this awareness in the middle of a frantic day. This is one of the reasons why setting aside some time each week to focus on oneself, whether in therapy, working on oneself alone, writing in a journal, or just taking a walk in the woods, is so important. When my schedule gets extremely busy, I use my time jogging as a time to tune in and work on what's happening with me. Maybe I recall my dreams, or create a new project, or get in touch with how my body feels. Without this special attention, it is too easy to go from work to the television set at night. We find ourselves in a routine, and awareness of what is happening inside gets tossed out the window. Therapy is an important tool to live life more consciously. Some people have been in regular therapy for twenty years, but being in therapy is not by itself the point. The point is to live life more fully and with more consciousness. Living life in ways that are truly satisfying and help us become ourselves in the fullest way possible is living therapeutically.

There are several important ways to expand our concept of therapy. First, therapy moves beyond a fix for problems and crises to help people live more conscious and satisfying lives. Therapy is much more than what happens during a session. All of life can be viewed as an opportunity for growth. Life is our teacher. As I heard one wise teacher say, you have a choice to live life fully and actively and learn this way, or you can wait for life to come around and kick you in the rear. I favor the more active, involved approach. Another teacher once said that we have a confusing over-population problem. The world is terribly crowded, and yet on the level of consciousness, almost nobody is there.

Small towns are an important place to help the world take some steps towards becoming more conscious. In our small town, many people are anxious to learn about themselves and improve their lives. As more people work in this positive direction, the quality of living improves for all of us.

There is another way of looking at consciousness that I love. Being conscious is like having a huge house with lots of rooms full of different furniture and different people. Most of us live in some of the rooms at the front of the house, but have little or no idea who is in the back rooms. While of course none of us would own a house and have people living in it with us whom we don't know at all, many of us are willing to do this with the different aspects of our personality. Getting to know these different aspects of ourselves and getting them in contact with each other is what this work is all about. These parts of ourselves we don't know manifest as dream figures, body symptoms, and relationship problems. If we can open those doors and get to know these parts of ourselves directly, we become bigger people—we have more of ourselves accessible.

We need to educate people through therapy and other means that they can learn to let their whole selves have a place on this earth, and teach them how to do this successfully. At this point, therapy merges with education. In all the great religions there is some call to know thyself. We have a long way to go to achieve this, and given our serious problems in so many areas, we need to make some significant progress soon. If we look again at the analogy of finding out who is living in the other rooms of the house, we first need to meet the other people, and then we need to get to know how to live together. Whether with parts of ourselves or with roommates in a house, this takes time.

Relationships between parts of ourselves take work just like relationships between people take work. If one sticks with this work, the end result is a more fulfilled and harmonious life with oneself and others. In the rest of the book, we continue to look at specific tools for developing this consciousness.

CHAPTER XI

HELPING PEOPLE PROCESS EMOTIONS

One of the biggest problems that people bring to therapy is not knowing what to do with a wide range of feelings, including sadness, anger, ecstasy, fear, and depression. Many visits to medical doctors are attempts to deal with feelings unable to be expressed or released. For example, imagine a woman getting a divorce. She is in favor of the divorce, but can't stop crying for days. Many men have similar problems after their relationships break up. Such feeling problems are quite common. In small towns, people often visit their physicians to get a medication to help them with a feeling problem. We see them when the informed physician says that medication is not enough and recommends counseling to work with the issues.

Learning how to work with our feelings is a basic area of growth. What does one do with sadness to help it complete itself? Some somatic problems are actually feeling problems. I once was going through a time of rapid change in my life where I wasn't interested in feeling much in my body, particularly any pain. I just wanted to keep going and not deal with all that was happening. At that time I went to get some dental work. The dentist made me a crown that was a bit high, and my jaw muscles went into terrible spasms. Suddenly, I was in incredible pain, feeling all of the different parts of my life that were painful, not just my jaw. One night when the pain was the worst, I was supposed to meet some people with whom I had painful relationship issues. They showed up at our house and I had so much pain in my jaw I literally couldn't open my eyes for several minutes. When we finally talked, all I could focus on was my pain. I began to tell them about my pain—my jaw pain, then all my pain in our relationship. At that point, the jaw pain left and didn't return for months. A few months later I was avoiding a painful relationship process, and my jaw hurt so much that I had to let out my feelings in the relationship and feel them completely. Again the pain got better. These were body sensations and emotions needing to be felt and released.

There are many ways to help people express their feelings. The simplest thing to say and the most difficult to do is just have them and believe in them. There is definitely a moment of choice when you notice you are having a feeling and then can do something with it. Imagine that you are feeling sad. What if, instead of turning on the television, you really go into that sadness and feel it in your body. Focus on the physical sensation of sadness. Often this is enough to let the tears flow. Or let's say that you are feeling scared. You can take a drink, call a friend to avoid these feelings, or really have them and learn about them. How do you experience the fear? Do you feel hot, cold, do you shake? Can you let yourself shake a little bit? These are simple ways to begin to notice and experience our feelings.

DEALING WITH ANGER

Anger is often the hardest feeling for people. Sometimes doing something physical helps with anger. I have helped teenagers stay in school and out of juvenile hall by finding a way to deal with anger. Popular ways include splitting wood, pounding on a pillow or boxing bag, getting involved in contact sports, throwing rocks or wood in the forest, and practicing verbal skills to express anger. I remember one boy who progressed from hitting teachers to pounding lockers. Later he was able to walk away from conflict and finally he could stay and process verbally. Many of these skills can be practiced at home. Like any art, dealing with anger requires practice to be perfected. Many people use their cars as private places to let out their feelings. Screaming in your car when going down the highway offers some privacy if you can drive and scream at the same time. Individuals process their feelings in the style that best suits their personality. Some people do best by hiding in their room and quietly suffering. Other people need to write or draw. I have a friend who can always release blocked feelings by writing songs. My closest friend in junior high school worked out his frustration on his drum set.

When feelings are present, why not let them flow? One of the problems with therapy is that many people only get to certain feelings with the support of a therapist. This doesn't work if feelings are ready to be released on a day and time different from one's appointment. I say, let the river flow. I myself am against pushing feelings out. Certain therapies access strong feelings through breathing exercises, pounding, or standing in certain physical postures. This could be helpful if a person needs to access feelings and can't reach the feelings on their own. For example, someone might be unable to cry and mourn a death. In such a case, any approach that helps the person release these feelings will be a relief.

For a more regular self-maintenance program, it can be helpful to express feelings as they arise naturally. Have a bad day at work? Find a way to consciously release those feelings, rather than taking them out on yourself, at the local bar, or on your spouse or child or dog. Give yourself a therapy session at home—go to your private space and let loose with whatever wants to come out. This is also a useful tactic during a fight. Let's say you are really in a terribly upset mood with your partner and just about to explode. Why not assess for a minute if this is really what you want to do. Are the feelings with your partner, or are they perhaps with someone else, or with yourself? Are they leftover feelings from last night's dream? If so, why not release them yourself? At home we are lucky to have a separate space where I see clients. I have saved myself a lot of relationship grief by giving myself a session in that room. It is also soundproof enough that the only ones who hear me are the horses, so I can really let go. If the feelings are really with our spouse, or with a child or a friend, it is useful to deal with them directly, but it is a relief not to have to work something out with a person if the river isn't flowing that way.

In *Co-Dependent No More,* Melody Beattie lists several assumptions that keep people from expressing their anger. They include:

- It's not okay to feel angry.
- Anger is a waste of time and energy.
- We shouldn't feel angry when we do.
- We'll lose control and go crazy if we get angry.
- People will go away if we get angry at them.
- Other people should never feel anger toward us.
- If others get angry at us, we must have done something wrong.
- If other people are angry at us, we made them feel that way and we're responsible for their feelings.
- If we feel angry, someone else made us feel that way and that person is responsible for fixing our feelings.
- If we feel angry at someone, the relationship is over and that person has to go away.
- If we feel angry at someone, we should punish that person for making us feel angry.
- If we feel angry at someone, that person has to change what he or she is doing so we don't feel angry any more.
- If we feel angry, we have to hit someone or break something.
- If we feel angry, we have to shout and holler.
- If we feel angry at someone, it means we don't love that person any more.
- If someone feels angry at us, it means that person doesn't love us any more.
- Anger is a sinful emotion. It's okay to feel angry only when we can justify our feelings.

Like all myths, on occasions some of these reasons may have some truth, but most often they do not. However, many of us live as if these are facts. There are similar assumptions about other feelings, such as: men who cry are weak, men shouldn't be scared, women shouldn't be too aggressive, if you go into your sadness you might not be able to function, and so forth.

POSITIVE EFFECTS OF EXPRESSING FEELINGS

I have created a summary of positive effects of expressing feelings to balance some of our ideas about negative effects.

Finding a healthy way to express feelings is good for your health and can prevent psychosomatic ailments. There is evidence linking emotional factors to a range of physical problems including asthma, arthritis, cancer, ulcers, allergies, and other conditions.

One of the most dramatic improvements I have seen was with a woman who came to one of my classes when I first started teaching dreamwork. She had developed a problem in one of her legs when she was taking her daughter to meet a plane. Suddenly, she couldn't walk on one leg. She was scheduled for surgery the following week. We worked on her feelings about her daughter, and as the anger and hurt came out, her leg suddenly got better.

Another time a man carried his wife, who was a client of mine, into the office. She was having such terrible back pain she couldn't walk. After releasing a lot of feelings and making some decisions about a job situation, she walked out of the office. Another time I was working with a teenager who was scheduled for surgery for an abdominal problem. We worked on this symptom. She began pounding on a pillow and letting out incredible rage against her father. That week when she went to the doctor for a pre-surgery exam, the condition was gone and didn't return. This instant disappearance of a symptom is certainly not the norm—sometimes it takes a very long time for psychological work like this to help move physical symptoms, in cooperation with physicians, chiropractors, and other healing practitioners. Sometimes conditions don't get better at all, but these few cases are powerful enough to point out the positive effects of emotional expression.

Expressing emotions can help make for rich and interesting relationship experiences, and emotions are an important part of forming intimate connections. In fact, for many people, being able to freely express their feelings with someone is the turning point in having a deeper connection.

People who can express their emotions free up energy to do other things in life. Being open with one's feelings is often an important ingredient in accessing one's own creativity.

People who are able to express their emotions freely are less likely to become addicted to alcohol or drugs. Many of the addicts I have worked with needed their drugs or alcohol to help them deal or not deal with difficult feelings.

People who can process emotions deal more constructively with grieving. Losing people close to you through someone dying or the death of a relationship is difficult for everyone, but people who can feel and express their feelings handle these situations much more effectively than those who can't express them.

Those who process emotions regularly are less prone to emotions coming out in uncontrolled ways, so these people tend to feel more in control of themselves. This is in contrast with people who are without emotionality until they explode in ways that are inappropriate and cause pain and damage in their lives.

Many different psychological approaches emphasize the importance of emotional expression, including Gestalt, Bio-Energetics, process-oriented psychology, and Reichian therapy. In the 1980s, the concept of expressing emotions shifted from its highly elevated position to a piece in a more holistic view that emphasized emotional development as one part of a person's total development. For those who are quite developed in their feeling capacity, the growth process might take them in the direction of developing their thinking, or their physical strength and agility, or their spirituality.

Whether it is emotional development, learning to work with dreams, spiritual development, or developing the health of one's physical body, I have found people make incredible progress just by learning to value and give time and energy to the growing aspect of one's life. Once I was at a conference on different methods of working with symptoms. I noticed all the teachers deferring to the wisdom of one man, Sun Bear, a Native American teacher. This experience led me to study with Sun Bear and other Native American teachers whose traditions have a tremendous wealth of knowledge in the fields of healing body, mind, and spirit. Sun Bear teaches people the importance of keeping emotionally clear. He has a beautiful method that I recommend to everybody. He tells people to go out, preferably into the forest for privacy, or wherever you feel comfortable in nature, and dig yourself a hole in the ground. Then you lay flat on the ground with your head over the hole and scream your feelings and cry and speak whatever needs to come out into that hole. The final step is to take a seed, place it in the hole, and cover it up with dirt, therefore symbolically composting your negative feelings and helping plant something that can grow. I have tried this method and at times have found it very effective.

One time my wife and I were visiting another medicine man who told us that, in his tradition, people go up on in the mountains and scream out all of their pain. These healing traditions have helped people for centuries. The catharsis that goes on in a modern therapist's office is no different than screaming on a mountain. I find all of these approaches useful, and as emotionally repressed as our culture is, any or all of these approaches offer important ways to balance and compensate for too much importance placed on intellectual development and material well-being.

When I first moved to my small town, I met with a doctor who was known for his progressive views. He asked me how I could help some of his patients who were depressed. Most of the people he was talking about worked in the mills. When I talked with him about helping his patients explore and express the feelings in their depression and then to make life changes based on this work, he looked at me with distress and said "You can't do this with these people." The doctor believed in the old myth that if people get in touch with their emotional reality, they would not be able to continue in their present lives. He believed that I might help them emotionally, but only at the cost of their lives falling apart. After several years of working with people in situations similar to the ones he described to me, I find that his concerns were more myth than fact. When people are in touch with their feelings, they have more choices. They can make wholesale changes in their lives, or incremental changes, or no change at all. They know, though, what they are feeling, and this helps them live their lives in ways that give them more satisfaction.

For example, I'm thinking of a man who told me he didn't like his job. He even knew what kind of feeling the job tended to produce in him that made him want to change jobs. He did not fall apart and stop functioning. Instead he made some very intelligent decisions. He decided to keep working, since he had to feed his family, but to remain aware of his unhappiness and begin searching for new job possibilities. He began researching the outer job market and searching in his heart for a career that was really right for him.

There are many stories like this one. People who process their feelings are better employees, not worse ones. They take fewer sick days and tend to stay with their jobs longer because they don't need to leave just because they have some negative feelings towards the job or their supervisor. I am such a strong believer in this method that I have helped businesses set up methods for helping people process the feelings they have about their jobs and their co-workers and bosses. While the bosses initially feared that havoc and chaos would reign, what actually happened was that people had renewed interest in their jobs, and this new spirit was infused into the workplace. Emotional expressing and processing can be helpful in even touchy situations such as the employee/employer relationship. This takes special skills, such as learning how to bring up issues when you are in a vulnerable position, but practicing at home is a great way to develop the skills necessary for even more complicated interactions.

DEALING WITH BODY-CENTERED FEELINGS

Another part of dealing with feelings is to be aware of and find the meaning locked in sensations and feelings in our physical bodies. In process work we call this the proprioceptive channel.

There are several ways to deal with this when working on yourself. One way I have learned is common both to Gestalt work and process work. This is the simple method of feeling and amplifying the feeling. One way to do this is to get comfortable and start feeling what is happening in your body. When you find something interesting—maybe a tight spot, or a place you feel heat, or an itch, make this feeling happen even more. If you feel tightness, tighten more. If something itches, focus on the itch. If you feel heat, experiment with letting the heat spread throughout your body. In Gestalt, one just lets whatever happens go along on its own. In process work, there are some ideas about structure that can guide us. One can try switching channels. If you have a feeling, try making a picture of this feeling, or let the feeling go into movement, or maybe sound. Let the feeling move through all the different channels.

The difficulty with switching channels is why people often get stuck in one form of expression, such as always being angry, or always crying. People are stuck in one channel—they can hit but not say angry things, they can cry but not talk about their sadness, they can have lots of pictures of confronting someone but not do it.

Another useful concept in inner work is that of the edge. Let's say you are feeling your body and suddenly you feel an itch. As you focus on the itch, you start to feel a bit sexual, and then you get feel like going to make a phone call rather than have that uncomfortable feeling. This was an edge. Something became uncomfortable or unknown. Experiment with holding yourself at that point, finding out what exactly the edge is, for you. If it is right for you, try going over that edge, having those feelings, and finding out what they are about. I remember one of the most shocking pieces of work I ever did on myself. I started working on myself by just noticing what I was feeling. Then I started feeling scared, and suddenly I started feeling turned on sexually. It felt really uncomfortable, and I was about to go read a book to avoid the feeling, but somehow I held myself at this edge. Suddenly I began to feel the most amazing love for all the people of the world, for every human being on this planet. I was shocked by the intensity of the experience. When we work on ourselves, holding down our edges is important. Uncomfortable feelings will come up, and behind these feelings are rich experiences trying to come forth.

You can also work on your physical problems with this same method of meditating on a problem, feeling it, and taking it into other channels. Draw it, sculpt it in clay, or make visual images. Take the symptom into movement, or sound. Sometimes just working in this way can help symptoms improve. When material is accessed, understood, and integrated, whether the original material is a dream, a body symptom, or a relationship problem, the boat starts moving down the river again.

If you want to go even a step further in working with your symptoms, imagine that you were not the victim but the creator of the symptom. What kind of force are you who is creating the symptom? Are you a monster, a witch, a disciplinarian? What is the meaning behind the symptom? How do you want the part of yourself that is a victim of this symptom to change? Now you have gone beyond processing the details of the problem; you are picking up the deeper meaning behind your symptom.

Most of this work with body symptoms works on the dreaming level. The approaches I have mentioned help us to get in touch with, and unfold, the symbolic material present in our symptoms, and bring out the dream figures present. There are also several ways to work on the sentient level, the deepest

wells of experience and feeling from which symptoms origi-
nate. The theory is that by working at this level, we may be
able to give the symptom an alternative way to express itself.
One way to access this level is to start by meditating on a
symptom. The next step is to identify what is the most unknown or scary part of the symptom. From here, notice what is
the essence of that part of the symptom. For example, someone
with a breast lump said the essence of it was its hardness. The
next step would be to ask what is the essence of hardness; that
is, what was present before even hardness comes to mind. In
the case of the breast lump, the woman said being "immov-
able." This is where her description of the essence felt like she
had reached the deepest description she could come up with.
The person then expresses this essential quality in some kind of
creative way, either using music, singing, poetry, dance, drama,
painting, or some other form of creativity. This particular
woman made a dance of immovability. The final step is to ask
the person how they need more of this quality in their lives.
She said she needed much more of this immovability in her
following her interests in terms of studying and work. Most of
her time was spent on meeting others' needs, and now it was
time to be rock solid about her conviction to follow her own
interests. I found it most interesting that, when she went back
to the doctor, this lump that had been around for a long time,
had disappeared. The sentient work may have helped with this.

Chapter XII

Self-Sufficiency

Learning About Self-Sufficiency

Remember when I talked about leaving the suburbs of St. Louis and ending up in British Columbia at the Gestalt Institute? My experience there was mixed. I loved the techniques of this approach, its appreciation of dreams, and its emphasis on spontaneity and being in the here and now. On the other hand, the Gestalt relationship approach needed to move further into areas of sensitivity as well as confrontation. Gestalt relationship work was based on the philosophy of "I do my thing and you do yours." Thus, it was excellent at teaching people to let their feelings fly, but not particularly good at picking up where the other person was or sensing what level of feeling would be appropriate for the receiver.

Despite the fact that Gestalt training at that point in time did not teach me about expressing feelings in a way that worked for another person, there were many important points I learned while studying at the Institute. I grew up in the school of suburban living. I didn't have to cook for myself, didn't do my own laundry, and was in other ways taken care of. If something broke at home, we called our favorite repairman, who could fix anything. At school, we looked down on our fellow students who took auto mechanics, metal shop, and the other technical classes.

I arrived at the Gestalt Institute to find that it had a high value on self-sufficiency in daily physical existence. People there grew and preserved their own food and raised goats for milk, chickens for eggs and meat. People worked on their own cars, following the lead of the director who rebuilt the engine of his Volkswagen by himself. If you wanted to eat, most times you needed to cook for yourself. If you needed to keep warm, you could gather dead wood or take a chain saw and get yourself some wood. I hadn't planned on this. I could tell many stories about my learning—like the first time I tried to make my own food, the early disasters, and all the screaming when I filled the kitchen with smoke. Then my growing successes—my first pie, my first bread, and eventually learning to cook gourmet meals.

Then there was learning about a car—my Camaro wouldn't work on those island logging roads, so I ended up with a 1959 Volkswagen pickup that worked until the day I bought it. After that, everything that could possibly go wrong did, including the time it caught on fire. I had to learn to work on it, and while I never was able to do major repairs, I learned what I needed to do to get that car home many a time when I was stuck somewhere. I also learned other things about self-sufficiency. The first winter I almost froze. The plants in my cabin turned to ice before I learned the art of making and keeping a good fire. I learned to can, freeze, and dry food. I had never even cut grass—I learned to plant a garden and grew sacks of potatoes and baskets of cucumbers. I learned how to milk a goat. Everybody in town knew I took care of billy goats, since I radiated a musky goat smell. I had never gotten a job before without family help. This time I not only had to find a job, but also had to go through government agencies to get permission to work as a practicum student. Before I had a car, I ended up walking ten miles a day, sometimes in the dark, to get to work.

Over time, my experience of self-sufficiency changed. At first, I was terrified that I would die, but in the end I learned to survive on very little. Since I had grown up in one of the wealthier suburbs in the country, this was shocking. I learned about connecting with the earth through gardening and animal care. This change helped me develop courage and faith in the universe. When I moved to Oregon, I was able to take huge risks because I knew I could survive. I moved with about $800, no job, and no friends or acquaintances. I was ready to live as self-sufficiently as possible, so I rented a farm for very little money, got my garden in, began putting up food, and invested the first money I made in an old rototiller and food drier. I injured myself making homemade wine—the bottom of a crock I had sterilized with boiling water fell out, and I healed the terrible burns with plants and herbs. There aren't any scars on my feet. I made it.

This experience changed my psychology and my outlook on the world. I was able to get a job teaching dreamwork classes that paid enough to cover my rent. I began to use skills I had developed as coin collector to buy and sell coins to help make ends meet. Often I had to scrape together my loose change to buy gas to drive to town and teach. When my car broke, I did as much of the work as I could myself. The jobs got bigger—I had to pull out an old set of dual carburetors and convert to a single carburetor, a job I managed with help from a friend. Without these practical skills I never would have been up for the professional risks I took to do what I wanted.

RELATIONSHIP SKILLS AS PART OF SELF-SUFFICIENCY

Learning to grow your own food, cook, fix things, and take care of your own health problems is not enough for self-sufficiency. We also need skills to deal with relationships effectively. Process work offers a sustainable conflict resolution method that goes beyond the one-sided confrontation popularized by Gestalt. Additional helpful steps include learning to take a neutral position, to take the other person's side, and to understand the primary and secondary signals you and the other person emit.

If we can learn when and how to take our own side in a conflict, we are on a beginning path to resolution. It is also essential to learn how to notice when we are de-escalating, which helps us resolve conflicts. A final step is being able to stand in the place of neutrality, as well as on our own side and the other person's side. Part of self-sufficiency involves fluidity in the midst of conflict. The most amazing story I have about conflict work comes from my own life.

One day I was eating dinner when the phone rang. A woman asked if I was Gary Reiss. I said yes, and then she handed the phone to a man. He said that he was coming out to my farm to beat me up. I was pretty scared, since he sounded extreme. I tried to protect myself like a normal person—I said I would call the police, to which he said that he would be there before the police, or would find me sometime when the police weren't there. He sounded determined to hurt me. I tried other things, but none of them were working. In my moment of desperation, I remembered my conflict work. I had been taking my side, so I decided to try and move to a position of neutrality and then to his side. I asked him what I had done to deserve such a beating. He said I had been at a bar and had beaten his brother. I said that I didn't go to bars, particularly the local bar. He still was not satisfied with my neutrality, so I took his side. I said "Look, if I am the man who did this to your brother, I think you deserve to beat me up. In fact, I will hand myself over to you, but with one condition. We meet at the police station. If I am not the culprit and you try to do something to me, the police will be there to protect me. If you identify me, I will go with you and you can do whatever you are going to do to me."

Suddenly, the man changed his tune. He was quiet for a minute, and then said that he was sorry to have bothered me, since the man who had beaten his brother wouldn't be willing to meet him at the police station. We talked about our brothers, and I told him how I had protected my brother when I was growing up. He seemed changed, not only in his attitude towards me, but towards whoever had done this. He seemed to have moved out of the extreme place of violence that he had been in when he called.

I have used similar techniques during less dangerous confrontations, and I always find them helpful. Try these steps the next time you have a conflict—it's a great tool for your toolbox:

1. Ask the person first, if you can, if this is a time to work on the conflict.
2. Take your side, including stepping into the emotional part of your side. Go all the way in terms of stating your position clearly and with feeling.
3. Try taking the other person's side. Guess into their signals—say not only the content of their side, but guess into what they are feeling. Try through the use of feedback to be as accurate as possible in representing their side.
4. Step out of both sides into a neutral position and try to keep some perspective on what is trying to happen in this particular conflict.
5. Repeat any of these steps as necessary.
6. Try and resolve the original conflict that came up in step one.

CREATING JOBS FOR SELF-SUFFICIENCY

Feeling like you can stand on your own two feet in the world gives you the psychological independence you need to take risks toward becoming yourself. This becomes particularly important in choosing a career. The January 1990 Gallup polls released some interesting figures on work. Forty-one percent of the people interviewed hold jobs that they had planned on holding and made a conscious decision about. The rest hold jobs for reasons such as simple chance or lack of choice. About half of the group says that job stress affects their health, personal relationships, or their ability to do their job. Sixty-five percent said that, given a chance to start over, they would get more information about career options.

An article analyzing the Gallup data quotes Jim Green, a labor historian at the University of Massachusetts: "There's a real dilemma. The labor market isn't matching up well with what people are trained to do and with what they want to do."[20] Green says that many people view their jobs as "necessary evils." If the majority of people are not able to make conscious decisions about their jobs, many people are going to be unhappy with the work arena, a major component of life.

Part of the move into self-sufficiency has to do with re-accessing your dreams about career, and seeing how you can utilize your self-sufficiency skills to give you the psychological and material support to make the changes you need to make. I once heard Fritz Perls talking about releasing feelings, including anger, sadness, joy, and grief. He announced that the most difficult feeling state to be in and release is joy. Culturally, there is relatively little support for feeling happy. We are given a lot of cultural support to buy things that will make us happy, or to drink a beer and get a quick shot of happiness. But happiness is clearly not happening in many people's lives. If we look at two of the most important areas of our lives, love and work, we see that the divorce rate is soaring and that over half of us have jobs we did not want.

In small towns, people already know a lot about self-sufficiency. Many people who lost their jobs when lumber mills closed fell back on their skills and put up enough food to make sure their families ate while they made the transition to new jobs. These people knew inside that they would make it. If you don't feel you have the resources, abilities, and inner security to know you will live through change, then growing psychologically is just not possible—you don't have the inner strength to go over your growing edges in life. People who do have this inner security can move rapidly through different reactions to a situation such as losing a job and often end up feeling lucky that they have the opportunity to make some changes in their lives and possibly be happier.

Of course, for people who lose a job with little or no hope of future employment, the job loss is not an opportunity for

[20] The San Juan *Star,* January 12, 1990.

growth but a tragedy. Growing into a happier life assumes that the environment offers opportunities to grow and to make conscious choices. This is certainly not always the case, particularly for minority groups such as African and Native Americans among whom the unemployment rate is very high. For a group to have no options, either because there are no jobs available or there is no choice about which jobs to take, is tragic.

SELF-SUFFICIENCY AND SENIOR CITIZENS

As it grows in size, the group of senior citizens is gaining attention. We have seen that, for many people, retirement just doesn't fit with who they are. Either they are ready to retire before they reach a mandatory retirement age, or they are far from being emotionally or physically ready to retire when the retirement age comes along. Mandatory policies treat everyone the same, but some people have the vitality of a twenty-five-year-old at sixty-five, and others are ready to die at sixty-five. One of the options for seniors is to use their time to develop their self-sufficiency skills both to feel constructive and to supplement their income. I have worked with a number of senior citizens who go through a process of finding what they can do on their own, now that society has said that they are no longer productive.

I recently met an interesting man from whom I bought a saddle. He told that he had been a company foreman for many years. When he retired, he remembered that his father had taught him and his brothers how to make saddles, bridles, and other leather horse equipment. This man went back to those skills. He buys old saddles and fixes them up, and makes some of his own equipment. His prices are much better than the big stores, and his products are of superior quality. This is a success story in self-sufficiency.

Along this line, there are craft stores in my town that market items such as dolls, clothes, quilts, pillows, woodwork, and the art of senior citizens. Many fast-food restaurants hire senior citizens for hard-to-fill positions. While outside employment is a good option, people who can create their own scene are really lucky. Going back to work at a fast-food place for minimum wage at age sixty-five may be choice for one person and desperation for another.

CREATING YOUR OWN JOB

I believe in people creating their own businesses and learning to be their own bosses if this is right for their personalities. When I first left the Gestalt Institute, I expected to get one of the jobs I had heard about at social work school. Instead I found myself unemployed. I lived in Miami, Florida, with relatives for awhile and then in St. Louis before moving to Oregon. I worked as a gardener, landscaper, cook, and caterer. I remembered my ability to survive as a coin dealer, a hobby I had dabbled in. I began offering classes in Gestalt therapy and in dreamwork. I found myself forced to rely on talents I hadn't considered salable before.

I talk to many people who hate their jobs and who also have skills and talents they don't use or have never considered using as a way to make a living. One client of mine always wanted to write books. When she finally let herself try, she was published. Several years ago my wife and I met a couple who needed work. We offered them work doing our fencing, then cleaning stalls. They tried to start a company making a food product, but this wasn't successful. Then they started making jewelry in a special style made in countries other than the United States. Their jewelry caught on, and this couple did quite well. Other friends made and marketed kaleidoscopes and other crafts. Several of my former clients have become therapists, since they have been helping people all their lives and it is what really matters to them.

For some people, working full-time for someone else just isn't right. In my therapy clinic, we attempt to integrate the advantages of self-employment into our workplace. Feeling self-employed often helps people feel interested in, and devoted to, what they are doing. For example, if I have control over my time, I don't mind working for someone, and when I have some control over my time I don't mind working far more than forty hours a week. We encourage employees to take time off when they need it, to create their own work schedules, and to be as autonomous as possible. The only employee who has to be on a regular schedule is the office manager, and she modifies the hours to meet her own schedule. One of our male therapists took a three-month paternity leave. We try to create an environment where employees can freely process their relationship issues with each other without repercussions. When someone wants more money or benefits we sit together, work out the feelings around the issue, and come to some resolution. People have maximum input into the changes we make, from remodeling the physical building to deciding what groups to offer. This is an attempt to integrate the models of a traditional workplace with the advantages of being self-sufficient and self-employed.

BASIC STEPS OF SELF-SUFFICIENCY

The following are basic steps to becoming more self-sufficient.

1. Learn some basic skills that you don't know—maybe you have relied on your spouse to change the car oil, or mend a piece of clothing. Try to expand your knowledge into new areas. Community colleges and other night school programs are great resources.

2. Include psychological skill building in your learning. You might take a class on how to be assertive, or how to deal with stress.

3. Ask yourself what other people can do that you would like to be able to do for yourself and develop these skills.

4. Learn to plant a garden and put up food. Given the worldwide climate changes, you never know when you may need to grow your own food. Also, as more and more people are becoming aware, most of the food available in stores is so full of pesticides, herbicides, fungicides, preservatives, coloring, and other chemicals that eating it has its own health risks.

It's a step towards self-sufficiency to grow your own food organically. We live on an organic farm and grow vegetables and fruit with only goat manure, compost, and liquid seaweed and fish emulsion as additives to the soil. We have enough frozen apple juice for most of the year, and we make our own tomato sauce, pesto, applesauce, pickles, and jellies. As it becomes easier to buy organic products, we are slowing down on our food production, but the knowledge is there if we need it. In most places in the country where there are few organic products, or where the cost of these products is high and quality low, or both, growing your own is very important.

I have noticed tremendous changes in my own health since I eat this way, particularly in how much energy I have. Going to the doctor is a rarity, whereas, growing up, it was a common phenomenon. Without going into a whole section on nutrition, I can't emphasize enough how important taking care of your physical body is to development. It is a goal unto itself, and feeling good physically is a key part in feeling good emotionally. Mind and body are intricately linked; both need attention and feed each other.

For thousands of years, our bodies survived on natural foods. Nowadays, our bodies have become toxic waste dumps, since we weren't designed to process all the chemicals we eat. I will never forget a talk I had with a Native American man. He said that growing up, he ate the old way, with a diet of berries, roots, fresh salmon, and deer. His teeth were healthy. He didn't need dentists or doctors. Now his children live on Coca-Cola and junk foods. He had just come back from taking his daughter to the dentist again for massive dental work. Junk food tastes good until you consistently eat natural foods for awhile. Then you can't go back. Try switching over to natural foods— no chemicals, just foods. It may help your independence from the medical system.

A Native American medicine man I know once said that we think what we do to nature is separate from ourselves. We think we can poison insects and it doesn't affect us. But it does.

Whatever we do to nature we do to ourselves, since we are part of the natural chain. Maybe it doesn't affect us at the same rate as the bugs, but it accumulates. Whatever we do to one part of nature comes back to us. Remember that we are still nature's creatures. Try to eat like you are part of nature, not a machine that needs chemicals to run on. If we keep feeding ourselves chemicals, it is easier to start feeling like a machine instead of human being.

5. If you are not happy with the work you are doing, make a creative project out of exploring options. What would you really like to be doing and what would it take to do that? Find out if it is possible. Not that risks aren't involved, but is it possible? Check out the abilities you have, and your hobbies, your interests. Could any of them become a part- or full-time source of livelihood? Check out options at work. If you need more time, find out if working half-time or job sharing is possible. I have had a number of clients save their jobs and themselves by getting their employer to agree to job sharing and to understand that it can offer the employer many benefits. Check out whether you could do with less money and more time, or if you could use time off to supplement your income. Make long-term plans towards career change. Work on the psychology of your job. Could you approach it with a different attitude that might work better for you?

For example, I once worked with a schoolteacher who was exhausting herself by being such a thorough planner. We started experimenting with her trying to teach without so much planning, and without having to be so perfect. Attitude changes like this can make a huge difference in working conditions. If you are happy at work, how could you enjoy your work even more? How might you help your workplace become a better place for others? Self-sufficiency allows you to take more risks to make changes in all areas.

6. Another area in which I have seen people need to fall back on their self-sufficiency is when they are trapped in abusive relationships. I have seen women who are in severe physi-

cal danger in their relationships who are afraid to leave because it is still hard for women to survive economically in this culture, particularly as single parents. Helping them become more self-sufficient can help them feel free to leave.

NATIVE AMERICAN WISDOM ABOUT SELF-SUFFICIENT LIVING

Native Americans were ahead of the rest of us in self-sufficient living. They made their own houses, processed their own food, healed themselves with their own medicine, and knew how to barter for what was needed, all in an ecologically sound way. When the buffalo was killed, all parts were used for something. Sun Bear and the Bear Tribe teach a lot about self-sufficient living. His book, *The Bear Tribe's Self-Reliance Book* teaches basic philosophy and practical skills for self-sufficient living.

These are not only survival skills—living simply is nourishing for one's soul. Spiritual traditions, from Catholic monasteries to Zen centers, emphasize the importance not only of prayer and meditation but also of simple physical work. When I first got my practice going, I spent a lot of time working in the schools in this small town I have written so much about. I liked the job and was finally making a decent living. After a few years I was ready to move on to something else. I wanted to train therapists, to give seminars, and to study more. All of this required travel, which prevented me from being at the schools. Many people told me not to let go of this work, but I knew I could live more simply for a while if necessary. I took the risk. My career grew in the direction I wanted, and our agency has an excellent relationship with the schools, perhaps even better than before. Sun Bear calls finding what you want to do in life and going for it, "following your path of power." Mindell calls this following your path of heart. Following our true callings often makes us not only more self-sufficient, but happier.

It is easy to block out our unhappiness, put ourselves on remote control, and just keep going. Turn on the television, turn on the beer tap, and turn off to life. It is very possible to begin to reverse this trend, to turn on to life and all its possibilities again. A base of self-sufficiency is one way to do this. Another is recalling your goals and dreams, and seeing how close or far away you are from fulfilling them. It is easy to become one of the living dead, living life without your heart in it. Giving up on your unrealistic dreams can be useful, but giving up on all of your dreams could be deadly. Your physical body may live for years, but living a life without much spirit and excitement and vitality is a shame, when life is so short and offers us so much potential richness and growth. Make sure your path of livelihood is a path of heart.

CHAPTER XIII

DREAMS

GETTING IN TOUCH WITH YOUR DREAMS

Dreams deserve a whole book, for there is much to be gained through working with them. Honoring one's dreams by affirming their importance makes a huge difference. Just making a decision to write down your dreams when you wake up in the morning has helped many people to suddenly have a rich dream life. Another way to honor your dreams is to share them with another. In many of the Native American and other tribal cultures such as the Huichol in Mexico, Australian Aboriginals, and the Senoi of Malaysia, dreaming plays a crucial role not only in the life of the individual but in the life of the tribe itself.

Brent Secunda, who teaches in the Huichol tradition, tells people about waking in the morning and telling their dreams to a fire. Amy Lee, from the Iroquois tradition, teaches how to use pantomime with dreams, as the Iroquois do on certain important occasions. The Senoi people had dream-sharing groups in the morning. When I lived at the Gestalt Institute we shared around the breakfast table. I often share dreams in the morning with my family. Letting the dreaming part of you know how important it is often encourages this part to become more conscious.

TECHNIQUES OF DREAMWORK

Let's say you honor your dreams, and you share them, and you want to know more about what they mean. There are many ways to work on your dreams. One is just to guess at the meaning of the dream when you first wake up. Use your intuition. The more you practice, the more accurate you become. Eventually, you become so close to your dreams that you may know what they mean automatically. Another technique I call "holding the dream in awareness." This involves keeping the dream in one's mind during the day and seeing if anything that happens helps unravel the meaning of the dream. Maybe you wake up with a certain feeling that becomes clearer during the day. From this feeling, the dream becomes clear. Similarly, staying in touch with the dream during the day may help you become aware of the feelings that the dream is based on. Sometimes I just turn the dream over and over in mind during the day, and there will suddenly be an "aha" experience of total understanding. Some big dreams I work on and hold onto for years, and I find that their themes come up over and over again.

For example, when I was at the Gestalt Institute years ago, I had the following dream. I was at my grandparents' house, circling their aboveground swimming pool. Suddenly, a large bear appears. It flashes from black to white, and I don't know what to do with it. I try to hit it with a board, and this doesn't work. Finally I try to feed the bear, but all I can find is a rubber chicken, so I start throwing rubber chickens to the bear. I worked for years by myself, and with help, to understand this dream. I learned over the years that the dream meant that my own personal power and strength, coming through in the context of my family, was scaring me. I tried to hold off these more primitive feelings with ideas, with worrying, with all kinds of tactics, until I learned to feed this power that was both yin and yang, that flashed from light to dark, that was the totality of the Self. James Hillman talks in *Dream Animals* about the importance of dreams in which nature comes through. He says that it is important not only to understand these dreams but also to go into the deep experience of the animals. This dream was also the beginning of going deeper into studying different shamanistic approaches to working with people. In shamanism, such a dream would be considered an encounter with the ally. One of the first times I worked on this dream was at a seminar with Arnold Mindell. I had an incredible experience as I shape-shifted and felt myself become bearlike. Mindell threw me a plum in the middle of the work, and I ate it like I imagined a bear would, stepping deeply into the experience of the dream.

The theme reappeared when I met my present wife. At that time, I dreamed that the solution to our fighting, which we did a lot at the beginning of our relationship, was to go where the bears feed on blackberries, where there was a lot of nourishment, and there we could both find all the nourishment that we needed. The man who told us this was a large, peaceful, bear of a man. In the earlier dream, I am first confronting this energy and power. In the later dream, I am working on how to nourish that particular spirit in relationship. The first dream was about discovering this power and what to do with it. The next dream is a process-oriented dream about how not only to step into my own nature, but to find nourishment for both of us, myself and my wife. Also here, the bears are not seen as threatening, but as showing the direction of nourishment, eating wild blackberries and looking for nourishment in nature and in the wild.

There are many specific techniques for working with dreams. Gestalt therapists "Gestalt" a dream, beginning by telling the dream as if it is happening in the present tense. The next step is to become different parts of the dream. Don't analyze, but simply become. If you dream of a bear, become the bear, be a bear and find out about this part of yourself. Then you can role switch and dialogue with the part. In my bear dream, I might go back and forth between myself and the bear and say, "Bear, are you after me or not? Do you want to hurt me or are you just hungry, and what do you need for food?" In this approach there is usually some "aha" experience when you quickly get it. As one of my Gestalt teachers always used to say, we'll figure it out intellectually later.

Another, more Jungian approach would be to study the symbolism of the dream. In our example, this would mean looking at how the bear has appeared in myths and fairy tales. By understanding the archetypal nature of this symbol, how it has occurred in people's lives and dreams for centuries, I might unravel its mystery. Jungian work also emphasizes working with associations to dream symbols. Associations are my personal, verbal expansion on a symbol. An association differs from a dictionary definition in that an association is highly personal. For example, if I dream of a jet, my personal association may be of adventure and travel. A specific kind of association, the "pop-up" association, comes from Mindell. A "pop-up" association is the first association that comes to your mind when you think of a symbol. My "pop-up" association to a jet is freedom. By putting together my different associations, I can interpret my dream directly, or weave the associations with my waking life circumstances into a story that helps me understand my life.

I start to do this in the dream on the bears and nourishment. I was associating to blackberries—wild, plentiful, free sources of nourishment of nature—and to bears—in this case, happy creatures with berries and fresh water, who, left alone by people, have no need to be fierce. I put all this together with my associations to this big gentle bear of a man who was always taking care of his wife. At the time, I wasn't able to put this all together and see that the way to stop fighting was to feed our natural selves, to honor the wild part of our relationship that shouldn't conform to societal norms, and to remember to really take care of my wife. If I had worked further with this dream, I might have been able to save several years of fighting—our relationship eventually healed the fighting in the very way predicted by the dream.

Another way to work with a dream is the Jungian concept of active imagination, which works visually and auditorially with the dream. One visualizes different dream figures in one's imagination, and finds out more about them through dialogue. In the *Jungian-Senoi Dreamwork Manual*, Stefan Kaplan Williams gives several ways of working in the dream experience while you are awake, including having internal dialogues with dream figures.

Other methods include carrying the dream onward—visualizing on as if the dream were still going, or carrying the dream backward—visualizing what went on before the dream started. One can also amplify one dream symbol by meditating on it and letting it evolve. This is an introverted way of doing Gestalt work.

Another method is dream incubation. There are formal ways to do this, but one simple way is to relax before bed and ask your dreams for guidance in a specific area. Lucid dreaming, based on cultivating a state of awareness that one is dreaming while dreaming, is gaining popularity. One method of dream incubation is to affirm that you will remember your dreams and that you will dream in a lucid state. In *Creative Dreaming*, Patricia Garfield gives various suggestions for how to work while in the dream state itself. One of her recommendations is to go ahead and complete what you are doing in the dream, while dreaming, even if it goes against your usual norms.

The Tibetan Buddhist religion contains dream yoga as part of its spiritual practice. In Tibetan dream yoga, dreaming is one of the paths to reach enlightenment. Fritz Perls didn't talk about enlightenment, but called dreams the royal road to awareness. Those interested in the Buddhist method may want to seek out a Tibetan Lama or other teacher able to teach these methods.

Process-oriented psychology offers some important concepts and tools for working on your dreams. Process work utilizes all approaches available, depending on the kind of dream and the person presenting the dream. In this approach to working on dreams, you follow what the dream is already doing; that is, you follow the process of the dream. We might start with associating to the different dream symbols. Then we can ask ourselves, what channel is the dream in? Is it full of visual imagery? For example, let's say I dreamt I was in a field of beautiful flowers, and I notice the yellow daisies and how beautiful they look against the clear blue sky. In this case, I might want to use some of the visual techniques from the *Jungian-Senoi Dreamwork Manual.*

Or, is the dream primarily about relationships? Let's say I dream about a conflict I have been having with my boss at work, and we were screaming at each other. Gestalt techniques, or other techniques involving acting and role playing, switching from character to character and having them interact, would be appropriate for such a dream. Another possibility would be to have an empty chair be one side of a dialogue, and you the other, and then switch. Maybe your boss is in the empty chair in your imagination, and you first talk to the boss in the chair, and then switch and become the boss and sit in the chair.

A dream that is primarily auditory, such as one where I first hear a bell ringing, and then the choir starts singing, needs to be worked with in the auditory channel. I might try making sounds and singing.

Let's say I dream about how touched I am by the gift someone gives me, and I wake up in the morning feeling choked up with feelings. If it is a dream with a lot of verbal content, I might try word associations to the symbols, using words to make the symbols more personal. It might be useful to go on with whatever feelings come up, perhaps from the starting point of feeling touched in the dream.

Often I dream something like the following: I am running in a marathon. When we get near the finish line, I suddenly get a burst of speed and run past the finish line to the cheers of the crowd. I am primarily in movement in this dream, so a good place to start working on it is by running, imagining I am in the race. Sometimes it is not even necessary to move like the movement in the dream. You can just get up and start moving, and work with whatever movements come up.

Other times I dream about what seem to be spiritual themes, such as one dream of being surrounded by quartz crystals and creating a ritual with them. The crystals were glowing with energy and I realized I was in some kind of vortex of power. I might work on this dream in a spiritually oriented way, perhaps by meditating or developing a ritual. After this particular dream I devised a ritual and felt tremendous energy when doing it. The basic concept of process-oriented dreamwork is to follow what is happening in the dream. Other approaches tend to have one formula—use word associations, or work with imagery, or make affirmations. The beauty of process work is that I get the meaning of the dream more quickly and directly because I am doing the kind of dreamwork that fits the particular dream.

We have talked about major channels that might come up in a dream, such as visual, auditory, movement or kinesthetic, proprioceptive or feeling, the spiritual channel, and relationship. Another channel is the world channel. I have dreamt, for example, about needing to become more involved in the ecology movement, and I am working on these dreams by becoming more involved in groups that take strong ecological stands.

Dreaming gives us a pattern for going into new and unexplored areas. Before we can live out new parts of ourselves, we first dream about the new direction. One way to look at our dreams is to ask what new aspects of ourselves the dreams reflect for us. Before I became a runner, I dreamt about running races, and running through the hills. When I actually began to run, the physical act of running seemed much easier, like I was riding the wave of the dream into physical reality. Within the dream itself, it is important to notice which parts are closer to our everyday identity, and which are furthest from our normal identity. Dreamwork helps us to identify with all parts of ourselves, including those closest to consciousness and those at various distances from our normal waking awareness. Often the part that looks like our ordinary selves in the dream is closest to consciousness, and also our judgments about the dream are close to our normal identity. Those aspects of the dream that seem most unusual, unknown, scary, and disturbing are important to work with, as they give us access to deep and unknown parts of ourselves.

For example, I recently went through a very tense period in my life and had the following dream. I was doing a form of meditation called Chi Kung, and a man came up who noticed I was meditating. He encouraged this meditative peaceful state I was in. I realized he really did want to be friends with me, although in the past this hadn't been at all clear. When I woke up I was aware of the different growing edges this dream reflected, including having less conflict and more friendship in my relationships with men, finding time to meditate, and leaving behind my tense state. My basic need was for more connection to my peaceful side, and my growing edge was to leave behind some old ways of being and enter new ways the dream outlined. I kept this dream in mind during the day and worked on where in the day I could enter these peaceful states. As I did this, I also got in touch with some of my old mental programs that spoke against taking the time to be in these places. You can look at any dream in this way, reflecting on where the edges are. Another way to work on the dream is to pick up the edges in waking life and to make changes there.

Dream material gives us clues to the mysteries of our lives. Whenever I get puzzled about my life I return to my dreams to find the path, the direction of the river. I also get feedback from my dreams—if I have made the right interpretations and the right changes, my dreams change.

For example, at one point I was dreaming frequently about being left. Person after person was leaving me—old girlfriends, friends, even my wife. I worked on the dream in many ways, but one of the most powerful was to work on taking over and becoming the one who leaves, the one who was plaguing me. There were some old friendships that needed to be left behind, and some old patterns that needed to change. I even had to threaten to leave some work situations where I was unhappy. Then the dreams stopped coming. They returned again when I needed more guidance to feel my pain about being left. The dreams changed again. When you are in the river of your dreams with awareness, you move down the stream and thus form a working relationship with your dreams.

Our culture doesn't value the dreamer much. In tribal cultures, big dreamers are often valued more than those who have material wealth are. Again we have a lot to learn from tribal cultures, for when it comes to valuing inner life, these cultures are way ahead of us. The issue of cultural support is of crucial importance. To become yourself often means learning to tread where the culture may be unsupportive. I was once speaking on a local radio program and got the following call. A woman said she had prophetic dreams. One time she dreamed of a house, and the next day she and her husband were looking at houses. She told him excitedly that this was just the house she had seen in her dreams, to the last detail. He told her to be quiet and never talk about these things again or people would think she was crazy. She asked if I thought she was crazy. I almost cried for her on the radio. This woman is like all of us—afraid that her creativity and her inner richness are actually craziness. We all suffer from living in a culture that does little to support certain parts of ourselves. Changing the culture often means having the courage to step outside the culture's boundaries. Maybe the culture will even follow your leadership into new territory.

PRECOGNITIVE DREAMS

This brings up the whole idea of precognitive dreams. Many people ask if dreams predict the future. I have had many precognitive dreams, and many that aren't precognitive at all but symbolic. As a person works with her dreams, she can begin to sense which ones may be precognitive. They may feel different, or there may be other clues. Many dreams will give you specific guidance or precognitive material, but often one can't determine the nature of the dream before working on the material. Then one can often determine if the material is symbolic, precognitive, about feelings one is having, or about an experience of the previous day.

If a dream is indeed precognitive, why not work on it and possibly impact the outcome in a positive way? You might work on it in any of the ways mentioned previously, or use your creativity and develop your own methods. When I was about twenty-four, I needed to find a new home, a place I could settle in. Although I had lived in Canada and Florida, the only place I had ever lived for a long period of time was St. Louis. I had a good intuitive feeling about Oregon and went to look at Ashland, but this didn't feel right and I went back to the East Coast. There I read about several places in Oregon, including Eugene. A while later I dreamed I saw a map and heard a voice say, "You are to move to Eugene, Oregon." I packed up my car and moved to a small town near Eugene. In this case the dream added information and supported my move. In contrast, if I had been thinking of moving to the West Coast and had a dream that said move to Mississippi, I probably wouldn't have gone. Instead, I would have worked on the dream symbolically, to discover what living in Mississippi would mean for me symbolically, with the hope of integrating the meaning of Mississippi into my life. Sorting out dream material and deciding what a particular dream means can be most helpful.

Most recently I have developed a kind of dreamwork I find simple and exciting. First, I take the dream and go back to the day before and find out where in the day I had some feelings or other experience that I put aside, usually because the material was a bit difficult or threatening. Then I see if this dream is an amplification of that feeling. If it is, I take the feeling more seriously and come back to it. For example, the other day I was with a friend. I noticed that she took more risks than I did at the beach. I found something painful in my slow, plodding style and didn't want to look at it. That night I had a long, involved dream in which my friend and I were both on top of buildings, one of my favorite places to be in my dreams even in childhood. She was leaping from roof to roof safely and gracefully and I was crawling, terrified of falling. This dream amplified for me the conflict and dialogue I was having with myself between my risk-taking and my cautious sides. I knew then that I needed to work more on this internal conflict.

Dreaming this dream forward would mean watching for the next day or so to see how and where the dream dialogue between these two sides played out. I would become more aware of when I was leaping and crawling within the course of the day, or be more aware of what happened in my environment that gave me more information on this topic. If we view dreaming as happening all the time, precognition simply means that we are in touch with something in our lives and ourselves before it actually manifests. The more we become aware, the more precognitive we are. We see the future present in the moment, and in our dreams, and life becomes much less shocking.

LIVING OUT ONE'S DREAMS

One of my ongoing dreams is to see counseling centers that support all the parts of the person, so the person who wants to be wealthy gets support, and the person who has big dreams gets support for that. I want the poet and the artist to get support, the people who want traditional marriages to feel at home, and the people who don't want marriage to be welcomed as well. This is a democracy in which each person not only has equal rights, but people receive support for all the parts of themselves. I do make a clear distinction between supporting the dreamer in someone who dreams of shooting a gun and supporting someone who might want to shoot people. A good therapist makes clear that it isn't all right to shoot people, but that it might even be possible to recycle some of this murderous energy.

For example, I know a very nice person who could never stand up for herself. She dreamed of murdering people with an ax. Integrating this side might give her access to her own power to chop through obstacles in her life. One way to work with this dream is to support her "murdering her own one-sidedness" in life momentarily. A democratic psychology is like a democratic political system. In a democracy, there are still rules and guiding principles, but there is free speech where every part theoretically has a right to be heard. This is the essence of this kind of psychology—any part can come up to have its say. What happens after a part emerges will depend on the individual and the wisdom of the universe. In the last chapter, we will consider how small towns can help further the true democratic development of this society.

DREAMWEAVING

Dreamweaving is based on the idea that all of life has a dream-like quality. We can view outer life and inner life as an ongoing dream, as a thread that goes from dream to waking body experiences, to relationship problems and world issues, and then back to dreams. This concept allows us to jump in at any point. Some people don't remember their dreams, or are so overwhelmed by what happens in outer life that they can't focus on their dreams. For a person like this, we can start with viewing life as if it were a dream.

For people who remember their dreams, we can weave the threads of the dream and life together. For example, someone dreams of a window that couldn't be opened, yet through great effort they pry it open. At the same time their relationship life, which they had been putting lots of energy into, begins to open. They suddenly meet two new people that they might be interested in having a relationship with. At the same time, they have physical sensations of energy rushing through their bodies. We can weave all of this together and talk about how they were like a stuck window, and how it feels to be more open, and the effort it took, and also find out what it feels like to be opening up energetically in their body experience. In dreamweaving, we can talk, do body work, or do relationship role-playing, since it is all part of the same fabric. We can weave together our dream associations, our awareness of what channel the dream is in, our awareness of edges in the dreams, and then take this information and weave it into the other parts of our life. We hook up dream material with our relationship experiences, our physical symptoms, and outer life.

One fun way to do this is through myth making. Myth making means creating stories that integrate our dreams and our waking experiences. For example, let's say I am in a tough relationship battle, I have a sore throat, and I dream of a roaring lion. My association to a lion is "the king of the jungle," and my pop-up association is unbridled power. Using this, I tell a story about a person who was timid in relationship. He couldn't speak up for himself. Then he met Jane who challenged him in relationship by being strong and speaking up for herself. One day when walking in the jungle, he ran into a lion who gave him a gift. The lion said, "You need to open up your mouth and let your feelings out with some freedom in your voice. Then you won't have to get those sore throats that make your voice so growly. The lion touched the man in the belly and he began to roar." That day I went back and was able to tell Jane with great clarity and strength how I felt and what I wanted. This kind of weaving can be done as a more formal exercise or as a part of everyday life as people learn to see all of life as a dream.

CHAPTER XIV

RELATIONSHIPS

WORKING ALONE AND WITH A THERAPIST

Intervening in a relationship conflict requires a tremendous act of awareness by at least one of the partners. Relationship is one of the most difficult areas to work without outside help. It is often nearly impossible to stay aware when you are in a relationship process. In most relationship conflicts, no one is reflecting, attempting to work things out, or picking up subtle signals. Instead, we are usually simply reacting.

Seeking a therapist's help is almost a necessity in this complex world of relationships. I know couples who have never seen a therapist, but too often they are resigned to suffering, saying either: "it's terrible between us, but we stay together for the children," or "we live here in the bliss of denial." There are many issues to work through in any relationship, but especially now, as society changes rapidly, the need for unbiased, skilled help is crucial.

My own personal experience, both with going to couples therapy and supervising therapists who work with couples, is that it is not easy to find a good therapist. The most difficult quality to find in a couples therapist is someone aware of the position they take in regard to a couple. Can they maintain some neutrality, or can they consciously side with one person and then the other? It is easy to become unconsciously polarized, and while taking one side or the other can be a positive intervention, if done consciously, it is more common that one side just sucks in the therapist. When this happens, people's relationships can be damaged more than helped. I have had many couples come to me where one person, or even both partners, is extremely reluctant because their last therapist was so against them in therapy that they never took their side. Picking your therapist wisely is very important, since primary relationships are an important part of life.

WORKING ON RELATIONSHIPS WITHOUT A THERAPIST

When we first met, my wife and I had unbelievable arguments that cycled for hours as we said the same thing in different ways and ignored our own and each other's signals. For example, after an hour or so, she would usually stop listening, as she was tired of my repeating myself. This upset me. I wanted her to hear me, so I talked louder and in more dramatic ways. She would listen even less, I would accelerate, and this could go on for hours.

I noticed several times that we were saying the same things repeatedly, but our awareness was not high enough to pick this up. We went on until we stopped from exhaustion, but only after getting to the point that we were ready to split up. This is the point where knowing how to work on our relationship without a therapist, as we now know how to do, would have been extremely helpful. Even the best therapist is usually not there when you need them most. The therapist is not in your bed when a sexual issue comes up, or at the kitchen table when you discuss who has spent what money lately, or at the dinner table when that difficult moment arises. This is the time for one person, or both partners, to call up their own internal therapist to help with the situation. If it is extremely difficult for a trained therapist to maintain some kind of neutrality, you can imagine how difficult it is for one person in a couple to maintain any kind of objectivity in their own relationship. Yet it is possible. Just as therapists can be trained to maintain their neutrality in couples work, you can train yourself to maintain awareness and some sense of perspective in your own relationship work.

The gigantic leap you must make is to become more interested in learning, in growing, in becoming intimate, than in winning at the cost of your partner's losing. This doesn't mean you need to be neutral and cool and non-combative all the time. It just means that at some part of the process you must be willing to shift into this other mode as well.

PRACTICAL INTERVENTIONS

Following are some practical interventions that I have tried out myself and with couples I have worked with in therapy. Most of them come from process-oriented psychology, and some are my own integration of different techniques.

First, learn to assess conflicts and issues between the two of you in the following ways. Ask yourself, "Is this a serious issue worth dealing with, or not?" Mindell divides conflicts into malignant and benign. Malignant conflicts grow worse, spread and reoccur, and need to be addressed. Benign conflicts are little issues that come up all the time. Left alone, they pass in a short while. Just remembering this concept helps in relationship conflicts. For relationship styles like my own, the challenge has been to recognize some issues as benign and just let them be, rather than starting a big scene over something that really doesn't matter much. For others with a different style, the trick would be to pick up on where the person is avoiding dealing with real issues that just get worse.

For example, I have worked with several men who consistently avoid the same issue until their relationship is ready to blow up. Some men are reluctant to agree to their partner's wishes to have children. They don't work on changing their position until their partner is ready to leave. Changing this pattern involves developing more awareness about both their outer relationships with women and their inner relationships with themselves—working with the child within. Some men decide to leave and never have children, and others stay and become successful fathers.

Once you decide to work on an issue, there are many useful steps. One is to try some kind of role reversal, as either inner work or role-playing. The theory behind this is that our partners carry to some degree parts of our own secondary processes. In other words, we are each other. Let's say I am organized and my partner scattered, and their being scattered drives me crazy. How much of this effect on me is a result of my not being able to integrate my own being scattered? How scattered is my partner actually, and how much do I project on them? To work on such an issue, I might notice a part of my partner's behavior that is really irritating me. Before getting into a conflict with them over this behavior, I might try pretending that I am them, role-playing the behavior that irritates me, and asking myself how I might need to be more like this.

Just carrying this kind of awareness usually changes the relationship process I am about to have. It's like the difference between target shooting with your eyes wide open or blindfolded. It is obvious which way your aim will be more accurate. This can also be done with your partner's permission if they are willing. If you see yourself as frugal and your partner as overly generous, try playing with these roles. Amplify the positions you usually take—if you are a bit frugal, pretend to be Scrooge himself. Have your partner exaggerate his or her position too. See if you can do this until the polarization is so exaggerated that the situation actually becomes humorous. Humor is powerful healing balm for the wounds of a polarized relationship. This means genuine humor that is not at the cost of either person, but emerges from the existential absurdity of the moment. It is also helpful at some point to try switching roles. If you are usually frugal, play the one who spends money like you have credit cards where the bills never come due. Have your partner be the one who is always watching and trying to keep the books balanced. You might then also talk about how you would like to keep up some of these role switches once the game is over.

Being stuck in one role can become tedious and painful for the individual, as well as wearing on the relationship. For someone who is frugal, knowing that their partner will cover part of this role might allow that person the freedom to go out and enjoy spending money, while the spender might enjoy that special feeling of seeing the checkbook balance and knowing that there will be enough funds to pay next month's bills. While playing with these polarities may seem insignificant, switching roles is often a crucial step in the development of a relationship. Playing with a different role provides an opportunity for couples to transcend their opposites and form a more creative union.

If we don't play with the polarities within our relationship, they may also cause us to drift apart. Think about magnets. If you put two magnets within a certain distance of each other, they attract. The closer you bring them, the more powerful the attraction, but if you stretch the poles too far away, the attraction drops down to a level where nothing happens. Relationships can also lose their charge. All couples go to all points on the electromagnetic spectrum with each other, but if basic polarities get too distant, it may mean the end of the relationship.

Another way to gain awareness before you go into conflict is to check your dream journal or try to remember the dreams you had last night. Let's say you dreamt that you were in a karate battle, and you still feel ready for a karate battle. Make a conscious decision if you want to take this energy into the conflict. Or, let's say you dreamt of making love to your partner and are still having romantic feelings. Maybe it makes more sense to follow these feelings, and on this day, to make love rather than war. I recently had an argument with my wife where I couldn't understand why I felt such a hard edge until I remembered a dream that related to my own childhood. My whole mood changed towards her. If we can protect our partners from the parts of our unconsciousness that don't belong with them, why not do so?

I recently had a dream that enlightened me about my relationship on a deep level. In the dream I was telling my wife that she didn't understand that whatever she did to herself affected me, and whatever she did to me affected her. Whatever I did to myself affected her, and whatever I did to her affected me. This is relationship—to wake up to the fact that we are not living in a vacuum, an island, but are part of many systems of interacting energy.

In a primary relationship, these energy systems are directly linked. In process work, we focus on three parts of a relationship: each individual is one part. The unit they form, or the "we," is another part. The "not we" that the couple splits off and fails to include as part of their identity is the third part. Part of emotional maturing involves recognizing the need to nourish all of the parts and the relationship between them.

Some relationships operate as if they are just two individuals, and others as just the we, or the couple. The most successful relationships seem to have a balance between the I, each person's individuality, and the we, connection and coupling. Following our dreams can help us have more parts of ourselves present and help us have more awareness of who we are and what we bring to the relationship each day.

LEVELS OF RELATIONSHIP

If you like to go deeply into relationship processing, you may need even more powerful tools. It is important to know how to identify what levels of the relationship you are working on, and what interventions work at what levels. We will focus on the following levels: communication and signal work, mythic work, systems work, and mood work.

COMMUNICATION AND SIGNAL WORK

Unconscious material often emerges in nonverbal communication, in the form of secondary signals from parts of ourselves with which we don't identify. If we don't pick up the secondary signals, we keep circling in our communication. One job in relationship work is to learn how to work with unintended signals. Most relationship approaches help with verbal communication. However, many of the signals that create relationship troubles happen at the nonverbal level, or are the subtle parts of the verbal signal, such as the intonation in a person's voice.

Let's think about a couple I worked with. The woman complained about the man's inattention. The man denied it, while at the same time looking out the window. This basic argument had gone on for years. Helping the man really bring out the part that is looking out the window helps him find out about a part of himself that he doesn't know much about, but his wife sees all the time. Bringing out these signals helps the wife feel that she is not crazy, but picking up on strong signals she receives daily. Then progress can be made. The different parts of the process are now available to be worked with.

Experimenting with following signals that either partner notices is a basic way to discover more about the background communication of a relationship. For example, if your partner accuses you of being controlling, you might want to explore ways in which that could be true. Or, if you find your partner looking down during discussions, you could explore together to discover what is behind this signal. This approach is a simple way to go more deeply into the levels of communication that, left alone, can cause all kinds of relationship troubles. Explored they can bring richness into the relationship.

It is also important to know what channels of perception are involved at each level of communication. We have seen that communication occurs in visual, auditory, proprioceptive (feeling), and movement channels. One of the most useful tools for quick movement in relationship is to try changing channels after a certain amount of time. If you are both being silent, try talking. If you are talking a lot, try moving together. Stand up and just move. If you need a format, place your palms on your partner's palms, or your forearms on their forearms, and begin making circles, then follow the movement wherever it goes.

What is coming? Could it be a dance, a chase, a collapse and cuddle, a wrestle and shout?

Another simple channel-changing exercise is to stop talking at a certain point in your dialogue, go inside yourself, and feel what is happening to your body. Make a visual picture of this feeling, and share this picture with your partner. You might also try moving like your image, have your partner move like their image, and try moving together. This intervention allows more unconscious secondary material to come up.

I remember two women doing this in an inner work class. They both had the same kind of imagery come up, and began interacting as two snakes. They did an incredibly wild dance, and one of the women went into a trancelike state. The other helped her through this by making very wild sounds. Out of this exercise, they recognized themselves as kindred spirits and became dear friends.

Exercises of going into other channels and bringing out secondary signals in addition to more primary verbal signals can lead to rapid breakthroughs in communication.

Mythic Work

Relationships are like big dreams that reveal their full meaning if we give them the time and attention they deserve. The level of meaning, both personal and mythical, is the second layer of relationship to focus on. This is the appropriate level of focus when couples go through crises of meaning in which they wonder what they are doing together. At times of great suffering and difficulty, many couples cannot stay together without some understanding of why they are together. The meaning may be something obvious, such as being work partners or family.

Other couples have a meaning that is more mythic and dreamlike. Some couples are warriors searching for a worthy opponent, or two people committed to enlightenment might need to wake each other up. For those interested in exploring these parts of their relationship, it is most useful to look at the first dreams and early experiences people had when they met. These big experiences give people important clues. I remember a couple working on their first big experience. On their first date at a restaurant, the man tried a magic trick of pulling the tablecloth out from under the dishes. Instead of the trick going the way it is supposed to, with the dishes returning to the table undisturbed, dishes flew everywhere. His future wife was both amused and disturbed by the mess. Many years later, they are having major relationship issues. He continues to be a wild, magical, crazy guy whose antics tickle her and whose messes have become increasingly disturbing. She is no longer so amused, since they have children and other increasing responsibilities that make messes more troublesome than they used to be. However, they both miss some of the original magic, humor, and spontaneity of their beginning relationship. Part of this couple's work has always been to integrate wildness and spontaneity with order and responsibility, all in the same relationship.

Carl Jung talked about parts of ourselves that we could only learn about through relationship, and about the myth of waking up in relationship. Certain parts of myself I can only see through your reflecting them back to me. I must see you so I can eventually see and own who I am, and you must see me so you can see and own who you are. These deep themes are also reflected in ongoing dreams people in relationship have with each other, and crises of meaning help bring issues and dreams of meaning to the surface.

For instance, when I met my wife, her absolute sense of order drove me crazy. My chaos on the physical plane drove her crazy. Yet we couldn't get away from this part of ourselves the other carried. A big turning point for me was when I dreamt that I had cleaned our refrigerator and put it in perfect order, and then a golden light began to shine from the refrigerator. Somehow I got it, and I am sure she has developed more ability to tolerate chaos.

Systems Work

The systems level is another aspect of relationship work. As we decide who we are in a couple, we also decide who we aren't. In other words, we define the boundaries of our identity as a couple. The rest of the world will then carry the reflection of the not we, or secondary process of the couple. For example, if a couple says, "We are not materialistic," the neighbors will be seen as materialists. It is often helpful to step further into identifying both with the "we" and the "not we."

Several times I have asked couples in trouble who they were. They said, "We are a couple splitting up." I then asked, "Who aren't you?" They said they were not a couple loving each other. Then I asked them a strange question, "What would you do if today were the first day you had met, and you had no relationship history?" Unexpected things would happen, like simultaneously leaping into each other's arms, or beginning a romantic dance together. The we was important, even if they were coming apart, for the loving was also present, and if they could stay in touch with both sides, their separation would be much less painful.

The idea of the we and not we has serious political implications. Racism and other forms of hatred are justified on the basis that we hate someone else, not us. A person or group is seen as different and we feel justified in hating or destroying them. In terms of war, propaganda theory states that a key to gaining public support is to portray the other side as the monster, the not we. For example, during the Vietnam War, the United States saw the Viet Cong as horrible. In the Gulf War, Saddam Hussein was seen as the evil that the United States had to destroy. One definition of a war zone is that neither side can see the other side in themselves.

We saw this dynamic in the chapter on racism. One way to avoid wars is for each of us to own that the other is also ourselves. While it may be politically expedient to hate the other, this kind of thinking leads to a world of war. Just for example, the imagery of the 1990s portrays Muslims as terrorists. In President Clinton's speech explaining why he ordered bombings in retaliation for attacks on American embassies, he went to great trouble to explain that the attack was not meant for all Muslims. However, the way movies, television, and politics feed this tension is dangerous. If enough of us could identify with the Muslim in us that we project outward—with the more radical person who could die for a cause—the chances of war might be reduced.

When I was in Israel in 1998, my main interest in working with long-term conflicts and hatreds was to see if people could experiment with seeing themselves in the other, as well as processing all of the different feelings and reactions present. Picking up the otherness is an essential step in peacemaking.

In relationship work with the system, we work to expand the identity of the couple by supporting the totality. For example, I worked with a couple who fought all the time. Having them in my office was like being in a war zone. One time I asked them who they weren't, at the moment that they were fighting. They said they weren't dancers. I got them to dance, and they did the most beautiful waltz. They were fighters, but also dancers. Both sides were beautiful and necessary for them to be able to relate.

Mood Work

Another vital level of relationship work is that of long-term moods in couples. Couples spend long periods of time in moods with each other. Some periods are up periods, where everything is all right and loving. Other periods are down periods, where all is depression and hell. One goal is to help couples be more fluid between these different states. In process work, the up mood, when people are feeling that their expectations and dreams are being fulfilled, is called the high dream. The down mood that occurs when expectations aren't met and disappointment occurs is the low dream. The high dream is part of the inspiration and vision that carry couples through the relationship. The low dream also contains important feelings that belong to the whole, such as anger, depression, disappointment, and sadness.

These high and low dreams are like cycles of nature. Getting stuck in a high dream may mean that couples are missing aspects of reality that don't support the high dream. Being stuck in a low dream may mean that couples can't process difficult emotions. The high dream is like heaven, the low dream earthy, and couples need both sides. A third state is no dream, or moments when things are quiet and neutral in relationship.

Individuals need to learn to work on their high dreams about each other. They need to know if their high dreams are being met, and make decisions about how they might be met in the relationship, and if not, then what. People need to know how to process the emotions and thoughts, including disappointment, that come up when their dreams aren't being met. Couples also benefit if they know when it is a no-dream time and they can rest.

Long-term mood work may be appropriate when a couple has sexual problems. For example, I might be working with a couple who are not having sex, but both people dream that their partner is going to be a great sexual partner. By going deeper into the high dreams, we might be able to work towards opening things up and having people get their needs met. On the other hand, some couples realize through doing this how far apart they are. In one couple, the man was dreaming his partner would always be there for him sexually. He wanted to make love two times a day. He finally realized that his partner was interested in making love about once a month. Facing this reality put them in a very low dream. She was dreaming that he would love her and be there for her forever, even though she wasn't sexually available. In her despair over his wanting to leave, she went to work on her sexuality. In realizing how much he loved her and how mood work deepened his love for her, he realized that more than sex mattered, and he became more patient. Over the years, both partners moved so that both more love and more sex could be present.

Here's another example. Fred and Lisa were a long-term couple with children. Lisa was always dreaming that Fred would stop drinking and start spending time with the family. Whenever she got too depressed, Fred stopped drinking for a few weeks and Lisa grew hopeful again. Fred was dreaming that Lisa was going to let him be the wildly irresponsible man he was. He was always shocked at Lisa's hurt when he didn't come home at night, had an affair, or forgot to show up for one of the children's big events because he was out hunting.

When Lisa worked on her part of the high dream, she saw that she was married to a man with serious alcoholism. She gave him an ultimatum to get treatment and stay sober. If not, she was committed to finding a man who was more present. Fred also saw that the woman he was dreaming about wasn't Lisa. Not only wasn't she all-accepting, she had been tough and was getting tougher by the day. Because he loved her and his children, he decided to change his high dream. He decided that he needed to work on his own childhood issues, his original family's drinking patterns, and his own mother's unwillingness to make a stand with his father. He went to treatment and loved his partner for caring enough to put things on the line. Working with high and low dreams is especially important in addiction work. In the above example, it was when Lisa went deeply into her low dream and really experienced her frustration and rage that she was able to move the system into changing.

WORKING ON YOURSELF IN FRONT OF YOUR PARTNER

Let's move on to further techniques to help deal with relationship issues. One of the most potent is working on yourself in front of your partner. In these techniques you pick up your own double signals or incongruent signals and amplify them. Here's an example. The other night I was out to dinner with my wife. I was talking enthusiastically about something and noticed that my foot fell asleep. I said to her, wait a minute, I'm going to let myself go to sleep for a minute, not just my foot, and find out what is happening. I realized that we were having a very serious discussion that had gone on for a long time, the kind that usually ends in a fight. I picked up that I was tired and switched to a more interesting way of discussing the same subject. We had a lot of fun and one of the most exciting discussions we had had in years.

It is challenging to pick up on our own signals. We are more apt to notice our partner's signals and bring them up. The trouble with pointing out someone else's double signals is that the way most of us do it makes the other side defensive, so they usually want to hide the signal more. In fact, it is much easier to say to your partner, "Give me a minute to find out what is happening in me," and then to bring out and show your partner your own double signal. If you are saying everything is fine while you are pounding on your knee, then pound on your knee until you can bring out into the relationship what this part of you is saying. You might say, "Everything is fine except that you showed up for dinner one hour late and I am furious about that."

It is possible to focus on your partner's signals, and there are useful ways to help bring them out. Signals are shy, so they need to be coaxed. Try saying to your partner, "I hear how open you say you feel to me, yet your arms and legs are all closed tight. That must be important, why not find out about it." Or if your partner says, "I promise you everything is fine," with clenched fists, you can say "I like those fists you make, do that more and also share with me what you are doing with them." This approach has better results than accusing your partner of creating signals.

CONFLICT RESOLUTION

In the chapter on becoming self-sufficient, we saw a detailed explanation of conflict resolution interventions. In reviewing this briefly, remember the basic steps of asking the person if they are available for conflict, then moving fluidly from taking your side, to taking the other side, to standing in a position of neutrality. Here is a brief example.

Once I was in a conflict with a motel owner. I was convinced I was right, for he had violated an agreement. An important point to remember is that being right doesn't matter much in conflict resolution. I first stated my own side. He said, "Don't you yell at me," so I stated my position in a calm and quiet voice. We ended up shaking hands, but if I had continued to raise my voice, even though I wasn't yelling, I'm fairly certain we would have come to blows. So I stated my position strongly in a way that he could hear. I also took his side; he was not thinking in the same way I was. I was thinking of the importance of keeping agreements. He was thinking of how to make the most money. Both sides were important, just different, and taking his side is a way to value both positions.

Many conflict resolution approaches emphasize the importance of good communication skills. This method also emphasizes good communication, and takes it a step further into the communication involved in subtle and nonverbal signals as well as obvious verbal signals. This method also works with polarities. In highly polarized situations, communication is often not enough—there must be methods to access and express material than is further from consciousness.

For example, in the conflict with the hotel owner, I heard his rage and felt something like terror underneath, although he was not expressing fear. If I had focused only on the rage, the fight would have escalated. In ordinary communications work, I might have said something like, "I sense that you are furious," which probably would have pushed us along in our fight. Instead, I guessed into the terror and talked about the struggles of trying to make it in business and the need to make money at every opportunity. This sense of his vulnerability would have been skipped in normal communication work. My whole adjustment to his being, my softening in content and volume, was about understanding his signals of fear.

Working on ourselves alone, addressing the levels of relationship, and doing conflict resolution can all lead to more depth and satisfaction in relationship life. These methods combine helping individuals and the relationship grow, together and separately. Different approaches work based on the couple, the situation, and the timing.

CHAPTER XV

SPIRITUALITY

SPIRITUALITY AND RELIGION

One of the key components to developing oneself is having a spiritual belief system. With all of the impermanence that is part of life, with the realities of death and loss, it is especially important to have a connection to something eternal. A spiritual belief system gives meaning to life and its challenges. Without this perspective, it is easy to fall into a depression. I have come to this conclusion in large part through my work with the dying. Facing death with openness to spiritual experiences can be a powerful time of learning and even ecstatic experiences. People who don't have someone to help them get to this level, or who are not open to it, often find death a meaningless, terrifying experience.

Much of spiritual development can be done at home, as part of inner development, separate from involvement with an organized religion. Organized religion is a big part of spiritual development, just as going to a therapist is an important part of personal development. However, here we will focus on what you can do for yourself spiritually. For many people, being spiritual means being part of an organized religion, but for many people spirituality is simply the way they live, or their own form of worship. Many people also feel themselves oppressed by organized religion. By creating their own way of connecting spiritually, they can skip the parts they feel oppressed by, and go more directly to their spiritual connection.

I have been exposed to a wide range of religious practices in my small town. I have worked with Jewish people, Protestants, Catholics, Buddhists, people into New Age spirituality, Jehovah's Witnesses, Seventh Day Adventists, Mormons, and fundamentalist Christian approaches.

In this chapter I will talk about common beneficial practices these religions share. Anyone can benefit from these practices, regardless of whether or not you belong to a particular religious tradition. Because I deeply appreciate the importance of spirituality, I am able to work with people from a variety of religious approaches. When people ask me if I belong to a certain religion, I usually say that my job as a therapist is to support whatever spiritual path a person feels good about and that I think having a spiritual outlook and approach is most beneficial. Most of the time religion doesn't even come up. But sometimes it does—people need help sorting things out. One of the most common situations I come across is when one person in a couple becomes a "born again" Christian. They often need help processing how these changes impact their relationships with their partner and children who may not be having a similar experience.

When a person has a life crisis and takes inventory of the resources they have, spiritual issues often emerge. I remember working with a woman who was dying of kidney failure. At a certain point, she chose to stop dialysis, feeling that she had simply had enough. As she neared death, her conflict with the church came up. Before she died, she had her conflicts with her religion out openly with her minister. She made peace with life and was happy with her own version of spirit and the afterlife.

A few days later, I was out of town and called the nursing home to speak with her. I was told that she was in a coma. The nurse put the phone up to my client's ear, and as I talked to her she came out of the coma. She told me how she had made peace with even more people and that she was in a state of deep love. We told each other how much we loved each other and wished each other good journeys. When I called the nursing home after I got home, they said that she died ten minutes after we talked, having made peace with the people in her life and peace with her understanding and experience of God.

Sometimes people have specific psychological problems that are exacerbated by some of their religious beliefs, and then we need to work on resolving the conflict between personal psychology and religious beliefs. Two examples come to mind. One was a couple in which a man was letting his wife beat him. He was a fundamentalist Christian, who believed in turning the other cheek, yet this relationship was leading him to become increasingly more depressed. The therapy was delicate work that allowed him to see saying no to abuse as an act of holiness.

I also work with many gay and lesbian people, some of whom have been connected with the Mormon Church. While their religion is a deep part of their family life, the church rejecting them can cause tremendous psychological problems. Such conflicts are a major reason for teenage suicide in teens of all religions. In cases like this, my job is to help people process the contradiction. For some people, it is right to quit the church. Others have decided to stay in the church and keep their sexual life quiet, and some decide to stay and openly fight the church's beliefs on homosexuality. To be most helpful to people in these conflicts, I need to stay open to whatever direction they choose. My job is to help them sort out the conflict and to help them come out of the experience in the best possible psychological shape.

SPECIFIC SPIRITUAL PRACTICES

People who have a spiritual belief system seem to survive and handle life's crises with less difficulty, whether the crisis is personal, a relationship issue, a medical problem, or an addiction. The feeling that one has some spiritual support makes a tangible difference. I remember seeing a client who had recently been told she might have a tumor. She was sure prayer would take care of it. She told me how often she has prayed and people have gotten better. I told her to pray for me too, since I had just had a minor injury. She promised I would get better. Both she and I felt better after the session. This woman was also getting medical treatment, and we worked on the psychology of her symptom, which had appeared at a time when she was having a lot of pain in her friendships and relationship life.

In contrast, I remember a man who was at the beginning of his dying process and was also not connected to any form of spirituality. He was depressed and angry and giving up while he had lots of life left in him. Through our work, he dealt with his resentments towards the church he was raised in and started to have some genuine spiritual awakening. He read spiritual teachings, meditated, and worked on himself. He transformed so much that he taught many other people and me.

I have seen other people go through life and death without a spiritual belief system; they seem to suffer far more despair and pain. One big question I wonder about is whether spirituality is an innate part of us that comes through our dreams and the altered states near death even if we say we have no connection with it. Research in this area would need to study how many people go into near-death and death experiences with no spiritual beliefs and stay that way, as compared with how many change to have some spiritual connection that they can somehow communicate to those around them.

Prayer is an ancient ritual that I have found helpful for many people. I myself believe you can pray anywhere—it doesn't have to be with a certain group, in a certain building, or with a certain leader. My own strongest prayers occur at beautiful spots in nature. Going to powerful spots in nature to feel the spirit is an important part of spirituality that has universal applications. I myself find spots in nature where I feel a special sense of peace, or feel a lot of energy and feel my own energy growing. I leave these spots feeling recharged.

People make pilgrimages to famous power spots worldwide. For example, in Jerusalem some of the most sacred Jewish, Muslim, and Christian sites are all within a short distance of each other. The Tibetan Buddhists have sacred mountains, and the Huichol Indians of Mexico have their sacred mountains and caves. Rivers are also power spots for certain traditions.

My wife and I visit holy places from many traditions, and I usually feel a special energy. In Switzerland we went to the shrine of the Black Madonna, and in Mexico we visited the ruins mentioned in Carlos Castenada's books on shamanism. In Puerto Rico we visited a cave whose waters are supposed to contain qualities of the fountain of youth, and in Oregon, I feel this special energy when I go to different hot-springs waters on Native American healing grounds. In India, I had powerful experiences as I sat on the spot at Sarnath where Buddha gave his first talk. At Israel, I find incredible spots in En Gedi, located in the heart of the Dead Sea area.

Many of us have special spots that are especially relaxing and rejuvenating, and we can use these special places to work on ourselves. I remember once observing a therapist suggest to a person that she work on a problem by sitting on a certain spot she felt was special and seeing what kind of solutions came to her.

Process work has developed a mini-version of the vision quest as a means to work on oneself. In the traditional Native American vision quest, a person goes to a powerful spot and fasts and prays for a vision for themselves and their community. In the process-oriented version, you either go to a special spot or walk through nature and notice what you find and what happens, assuming that it has meaning. One can do this with a particular question in mind, or just to find guidance in the moment. On one mini-vision quest, I found an old Coke bottle in the middle of some beautiful woods. I was wondering about my next direction in life; the Coke bottle pointed me in the direction of ecological issues—cleaning up the environment.

Sometimes my journeys have been more dramatic. For example, in Hawaii, which has many sacred power places, I went on a walking quest to get information about my health, since I had a terrible case of the flu. I saw whales and dolphins swimming in the ocean, and I went into meditation and could hear the whales talking to me. They told me that my illness was due to needing to let go of work that was burning me out. I spontaneously decided to quit some organizational work I had been doing. My decision to quit this particular project was shocking to me, yet I have never regretted it, and the flu left almost immediately.

Believing in some higher power, whether it is inside, outside, or both, is crucial to benefiting from a spiritual approach. In most traditions, the higher power is personified externally, in the form of a god. Some traditions worship more feminine goddesses. Still others recognize the higher power as inside themselves as well. The view that the individual carries a spark of divinity often helps people feel better about themselves. The idea of God within has been popularized by the New Age movement, but is also part of mystical traditions in both Judaism and Christianity, as well as Eastern religions. It doesn't matter whether someone feels this spiritual presence in Nature, Jesus, God or the Goddess; what *is* important is that they have someone or somewhere to turn.

RELATIONSHIPS WITH THE DIVINE

It is generally useful to encourage people to have an active relationship with whatever spiritual power they believe in. I have seen many people who have not been able to recover from a certain experience until they work on their relationship with God. For example, I have had clients who needed to express their anger at God for something that had happened, or to thank God for their blessings before they could feel good about them. One of the most powerful sessions I remember was working with a woman who had been through a string of tragedies. What emerged from her session was her declaration to God that this was enough, that she couldn't handle any more suffering. She wasn't going to take any more, and this had to stop. That was the end of this string of tragedies.

In most of these cases, I don't bring up God. Rather, people tend to say things like "I used to be a spiritual person, then I was hurt in this particular way, and I stopped believing." Sometimes, if we work on the relationship to a person's spiritual side, their faith comes back. I take the idea of an open relationship with God from Martin Buber, who wrote *I and Thou*. Buber talks of spirituality as an active, ongoing dialogue between the person and God. Not all religious traditions support having a dialogue with God. In many, God is a strong patriarchal figure like the stern father we never question. Our role is to be his children, seen but not heard. This method has one drawback—just as in families when relationship issues go underground with a stern father and the child begins to withdraw, in a view of God that demands a person always be silent, part of the person starts to pull back from the relationship. Just as open communication seems to work better in marriages, open communication seems key in people's relationships with their spiritual selves.

Many mystics view the relationship with the divine as a love affair. One of the key components of spiritual traditions is the use of ritual. Ritual is an important way that we make and acknowledge psychological transitions. For example, spiritual traditions and cultures help us deal with death, providing structure to take people through the grieving process. There is something natural and organic about performing rituals at certain times—they are created by a momentary need, and the successful rituals become our institutions.

CREATING RITUAL

One of the most powerful spontaneous rituals I have seen occurred after a good friend of mine was killed in an accident. She was a very spiritual woman who didn't follow any specific religious path. The approach she felt most comfortable with was the Sufi tradition, which incorporates many different approaches. After her death, her friends gathered in a circle around a giant tree she had loved. People began to offer songs.

First one person and then another stepped forward and spoke about what her life and her death had meant to them. Many stories were told and tears were shed. Then someone led a dance in the Sufi circle tradition. Someone offered a closing prayer, then people stood in silence before we began hugging and comforting each other. There were people of all faiths present, from the most traditional to the most alternative, and the simplicity and beauty of the service touched everyone.

Creating rituals for various parts of our lives is not only important psychologically, but also a creative and enjoyable experience. Just as a story needs characters and a plot, there are basic elements to ritual. To create a ritual, one needs a focus or purpose, such as healing, thanksgiving, or general prayer. Then there are the symbols—a special book, candles, a crystal, a wine cup, flowers, or other personal symbols. The ritual must be created and enacted, with its purpose clearly stated. The ritual ends with expressing thanks for the spiritual help received.

One time a friend called and said his son was going away to college. My friend asked if we could convene a council of "elders" for his son. Many men who had known this young man throughout his life came together to recognize this moment, to give him advice on going into the world, and to be available if he were ever in trouble. The most touching moment was when the young man both thanked his father and talked honestly about their relationship. Then his father spoke about the challenges of raising a teenager and about some of the mistakes he had made. Afterwards his son went off to play in a band. The transition had been made.

Our culture lacks ritual transitions for many events. For example, a girl's first menses, which is honored in tribal cultures, is not noticed ritually in our culture. I have worked with many women who need healing around the trauma of their first period. Many women were not told about menstruation and were frightened when it occurred. Others felt embarrassed, or were teased or rejected. We need ritual to honor this as a time of graduation and celebration. Teenage boys also need ceremonies to recognize their time of transition, so they don't feel they are alone in a difficult time. People can create their own rituals within any family and religious tradition.

Another area in which our culture has a need for ritual is around retirement. Many older clients have talked to me about how they put many years in on a job, but nothing was done for them when they retired. We need ways to recognize people's contributions to help them make the transition from work into the next part of life.

Anyone can incorporate several key components from spiritual paths. One is a commitment to awareness, which is a crucial element in a spiritual path. A commitment to awareness is a commitment to noticing all the parts of life and oneself. It doesn't mean accepting, condoning, or condemning, but simply being aware of all of ourselves. This approach doesn't go along with some of the more fundamentalist approaches that say to ignore the bad sides and pay attention to the good. Awareness is openness to what is present; it doesn't mean that people can't make moral choices, just that they are aware of the possibilities. Awareness is a philosophy of openness to knowledge, as opposed to fear and turning away. Some religions provide something like a road map, and suggest that there is only one road to take, which is the good road. The awareness approach notices that there are many roads, each with different characteristics. The moral element comes around choosing which road to take.

An alternative definition of morality is the commitment to being aware and to process whatever comes to awareness. Let's go back to the man who allowed his wife to hit him because he thought his religion demanded this. As we worked on his depression, a new awareness came up. He noticed that he didn't feel spiritual which, in his mind, was something like uplifted. He felt depressed. When he experimented in therapy with stopping his wife and getting angry at her, he felt better. This produced a crisis in his belief system. He had to make a choice between his identity and a spirit that embraces all sides, including being one-sided. Our work was to help him to a new view of morality, one that included awareness of his feelings as something divine. He was able to put the pieces together—he wasn't going to divorce his wife, he was going to love and cherish her and not hurt her, but neither was he going to turn the other cheek in the face of abuse. We also talked about how his not allowing her abuse might help him open her to her own spiritual development.

In another example, I remember facilitating a meeting in Salt Lake City. The topic was gay and lesbian issues, and the gay and lesbian community, many of them Mormons, and a group of therapists dedicated to trying to make homosexuals convert to heterosexuality attended. Many parents spoke up, illustrating a deeply touching openness to all sides. One father talked of his love and devotion to his religion. He also talked of his love for his son, and introduced his son and his male partner, whom the father said was also like a son to him. He said he loved all of these parts of his life, and while aware that this position could cost him his religion, he had to say yes to all of his parts. His awareness, love, and courage brought tears to many people's eyes. This is an example of opening to what is happening inside as the basis of morality, rather than following a prescribed model of good and evil.

CONFLICTS BETWEEN RELIGIONS AND PSYCHOLOGY

Some traditions allow people to determine which choices are spiritually correct, while other approaches dictate these choices. Still others offer guidance in one direction or the other but emphasize free will in choosing. Both society and religion teach us to notice parts of ourselves and repress the rest. As a therapist, I see that this doesn't work for many people.

Both religion and psychology hope people will act consciously and ethically, but they often have different means to this end. Religion stresses repression, psychology integration. Ideally, therapists can help people both to live their religious paths without repressing their psychological growth, and to work though their psychological issues and be connected to their religious path. A dilemma occurs for many people when their religion opposes their natural tendencies.

As people grow and change, their relationship to religion may change. Some people grow more orthodox or strict, some loosen up, and some people switch religions at different points in their psychological development. Some religions are more tolerant than others of change. In one religious approach, as people grow and change and move along the polarities of orthodox to liberal following of the teachings, there would be complete acceptance of this movement. In another tradition the person would be asked to leave the religion, or even ignored by the people of the church. As people progress in their growth, it is important to be aware of such issues as these, and to have help from other religious leaders and their psychologically based counselors in how to resolve these issues.

Another area of interface is between religion and relationship. I have seen both men and women treated in ways that verge on emotional abuse, but the person won't challenge it because of what their religion teaches. I have seen mothers not challenge the father about abusing their children because the religion says the father is the head of the family and the final authority. I have seen men treated terribly by their wives who refuse to get angry or consider leaving because it is against their religion. These are difficult issues, and the most a therapist can do is help people process what is happening. Therapists also need to take a stand around the difference between following religious principles, and allowing abuse. Therapists can help clients know the difference between the two.

Let's say a man comes to me with depression. All he talks about is how his wife does this and that to him. I can see that he is furious, but not letting out his anger because of a religious prescription against anger. I can point out his choices—he can take antidepressants, he can try other approaches in therapy, or he can try letting some of this anger out. What if the person is holding so much anger that they are suicidal? We process together what it would mean to let some anger out. Will it destroy too much of the person's connection with their religion, or will it help them to be more religious? Can they rethink and reframe the situation so that they can have both their religion and their sanity, if the two are in terrible conflict?

The therapist's job is not to undermine religion, but to help people find their own balance within a specific religious path. If we view spiritual growth as a process rather than a fixed product, there is room for growth as people change. How a teenager follows rules and how his parents follow rules are different because they are different—their bodies and dreams and needs are different. People's needs also change—sometimes people need the structure of something fundamental, and other times they have grown into a phase where the authority is inside. Sometimes people need to take the fundamentalist part of themselves and transfer it to other parts of their lives, and then they may or may not continue to be fundamentalist in their practice. For example, a friend of mine became very fundamentalist in his religion. Where he really needed his fundamentalism was in his attitude towards alcohol, where he had a significant problem. When he cleared up the drinking problem, he moved to a more liberal religious practice but maintained absolute strictness in regard to substance abuse.

Another conflict between religion and psychology is around attitudes toward the physical body, particularly sex. I still see many clients who have sexual difficulties that they trace back to their religious upbringing. The work in cases like this is to go back and have people become aware of what they have taken in unconsciously. This provides an opportunity to consciously decide which of these early religious beliefs they want to keep and which they wish to discard. Much more can be said about the relationship between religion and psychology, but in summary let me say that the two can be helpful to each other if conflicts are processed thoroughly and carefully.

HAVING FAITH AND COURAGE

Courage and awareness are two of the most important aspects of self-development, and important tools for going beyond the status quo in life. To risk awareness takes a step of courage, and once awareness is present, changing one's life takes tremendous courage. Most of our modern heroes are people who show courage and skill in outer arenas—astronauts, athletes, or film stars. One of the joys of being a therapist is witnessing people's inner journeys. Watching someone work through an addiction or struggle through a bout of severe depression is an incredible experience. Depressed clients have often told me they journey though hell. Facing one's worst moments and having the faith and courage to move on is most impressive, and these people are my heroes.

Living with awareness and working on oneself are part of spirituality. A commitment to grow and learn more about oneself is a spiritual commitment. A commitment to change the world also can be a key step to spiritual development. In one ancient spiritual tradition in Mexico, people were dreamers, stalkers, or both as part of their spiritual path. Dreamers were more introverted and worked on their dreams. Stalkers were world changers who worked with the world and relationships. Process-oriented psychology trains people to be both dreamers and stalkers, to work on themselves internally but to view the world as their stalking ground for developing their spirituality.

PART THREE

CONCLUSION

CHAPTER XVI

SMALL TOWNS AS THE WORLD

DEVELOPING A WORLD PERSPECTIVE

At the end of the last chapter I mentioned the stalker as a person who develops their spirituality through their involvement in relationships and the world. There are many ways to increase one's involvement with the world, from becoming involved in local issues to becoming involved at the international level. In this chapter, we will explore a way of looking at our lives as a microcosm of the world, a view that sees the world process in our neighborhoods and towns.

In my small town, I have seen a parallel to the conflict between the former Soviet Union and the United States, with two highly polarized camps. The alternative community moved to this area from out of state and founded communities, communes, and health food stores alongside another group of locals who had always lived in the area. Before I moved to town, some local establishments wouldn't serve men with beards or long hair. The two camps were isolated and polarized, with hostility on both sides.

Gradually reformers emerged on both sides as alternative people opened stores and got to know the community, and locals got to know alternative people through schools and community projects. Over time, the whole field began to change. Tensions were reduced, and then certain crises brought up the tensions again. Peace is a process. For example, polarities emerged around timber-cutting issues. There was tension during the United States war with Iraq as some local people paraded and waved yellow ribbons and the anti-war group met to protest what they saw as senseless killing.

I will never forget what happened when forces of terror showed up in our town. Someone burned a large white cross on the lawn of a Tibetan Buddhist center founded by a famous Tibetan Lama. When he was interviewed about the incident for the local paper, he expressed only wisdom, love, and compassion for all people. He maintained his own enlightened space and no more crosses were burned. In his enlightened space, he refused to see the cross burning as a polarity between the "good" Buddhists and the "bad" racists. He spoke for them and for himself, refusing to attach to the negative acts of the racists. He simply said that the Buddhist center would continue to follow its path. It takes a great deal of enlightenment not to become polarized when someone is attacking you. This is similar to the Aikido concept of not being there to receive an attack— famous masters say that when they are attacked, no one is there. If we can be totally fluid in the moment, if we can maintain such a space, something changes, even though tensions may reappear.

I sit on a committee that works to stop child abuse. Some people on the committee who now hold traditional jobs used to be very much part of the alternative community. Others are government officials and leaders of fundamentalist churches. This committee is not so different from the United States and the former Soviet Union coming together. The scale and significance are different, but the distance the two poles had to move to work together is similar.

Our town, like the Yeltsin wing in Russia, needs to unify the forces present into a new configuration that will work. One of the problems we face in continuing to move the local consciousness is that the area in which we live has serious economic problems. It is difficult in our town, as in Russia, to move people's consciousness rapidly if their pocketbooks and cupboards are empty.

There are many other examples of the interaction between local awareness and international issues. The Bush and Clinton administrations could have saved billions of dollars by talking with our local counselors, who know that wars on drugs don't work—repression, fear, and intimidation can only win short battles. The war on drugs can be won by making deep changes in the environment and the culture, but not by guns and jails. In our small town we have had lots of crackdowns—more police, marijuana busts, amphetamine busts, stricter rules at school. The drug business still flourishes. Private agencies and school counseling groups who hammer away at this problem in a more understanding way, working with the problems people have and stressing prevention and treatment, continue to make steady progress. Innovative treatment approaches that involve social change also work. These alternatives don't sound as simple and flashy as a war on drugs, but they work, while the war on drugs is an expensive and ineffective attempt at short-term solutions.

These are just a few examples of how social issues on a global scale are happening right in the small town. We can look to global solutions to find local applications, and look to local solutions to find out what may work on a national or global scale.

CHAPTER XVII

TOWARDS A PSYCHOLOGICAL DEMOCRACY

BRINGING TOGETHER POLITICAL AND PSYCHOLOGICAL DEMOCRACY

The physical development of the United States happened from the inside out. We started as a nation of small towns and farms, and became a nation where most of the population lives in large cities. Today, another wave of growth is happening, a wave of psycho-spiritual development. This wave could also gather momentum in small towns and move out to the rest of the country. Small towns have the same problems as other places do, with the advantage that the problems are within manageable proportions. Along with this practical problem-solving orientation present in small towns is a genuine openness to change.

People in small towns have gone through hard times recently. Farmers, particularly small farms, face economic devastation. Many of the industries that have kept these towns in business are growing less reliable as a source of income. For example, there are several small towns in our area that have gone into crisis as the timber industry closes mills. People who are solution oriented are open to many solutions during difficult times. Some people come to counseling when their life moves into a crisis phase; others draw on resources to change their way of earning income.

Openness to change is also often present in liberal, educated, people living an alternative lifestyle, but this group is too small to push a wave of change in this country. Other groups must be involved, and small town people may be the ripest for political and psychological change. This may sound surprising, since small towns are typically identified as conservative. However, when stability is threatened for an individual or a town, it is possible to be conservative only up to a point. To deal effectively with crises, we must embrace change.

The small towns I know are in the midst of a change process. Counseling can be an important part of fostering change, particularly counseling that takes a democratic view that all parts of the personality, positive and negative, have a right to come into a person's awareness. Just as good leaders must know whom they are leading, a person needs to know what parts compose the self. Many psychological systems teach that bringing up unconscious parts will create anarchy, just as many political leaders fear giving power to more than a small percentage of people who really run the show. However, skillful dealings with marginalized positions are what ensure the long-term survival of a democracy. If the countries in eastern Europe are any indication, repression works well for only so long. Eventually the minority power can become the majority. In terms of the human psyche, repression is also only a short-term solution, and skillfully bringing unconscious parts into awareness gives individuals a much better chance of having long-term control of their lives.

Thus far, we have not done well taking care of marginalized positions either psychologically or politically. Hate crimes against minority populations are way up. Out of our own lack of wholeness we oppress women, blacks, gays, senior citizens, people with AIDS, and anyone different from ourselves. We oppress all the parts of ourselves we have learned to distrust and split off. Going to therapy is popular in part because our culture offers little or no support for many different feelings. When a culture leaves huge parts of itself unintegrated, there is trouble in the psychological democracy.

As a culture we also try to repress the drugs people take to access altered states, rather than becoming more democratic and changing so that these states of consciousness are represented. It is much easier to throw a bunch of money into new prisons than to really take on the problems of the ghettos and chronic low self-esteem present as part of ghetto life. Psychology and politics are intricately linked. Effectively dealing with problems such as heroin addiction requires social change. In the meantime, we'll fund millions for the war on drugs, a war that won't make much of a dent in anything but some politician's popularity.

One way to attack the drug problem is to become more democratic psychologically. As the culture supports more different states of consciousness, the individual no longer needs drugs to access these states. Our culture has what I call a steady-state ideal of consciousness. Our current system runs at its best when people are pretty much in the same state of mind at least fifty-one weeks of the year. On vacation, one may get to briefly enter an altered state, and on weekends and vacations and after work, television and beer provide access to other states of consciousness. Cigarettes give people mild altered-state experiences, as does coffee. The cravings for other states of consciousness manifest in the incredible drug and alcohol problems we have. There is no war on alcohol partially because alcohol keeps the machine turning to some degree. Many a worker has told me having a beer after work makes the job tolerable.

The first solution to drug problems would be a democratic approach to different states of consciousness. Such a democracy would result in tremendous changes in, for example, how our workdays are organized. Some companies are beginning to build in some times for other states as part of the workday, perhaps by giving time for aerobic exercise, which produces an incredible altered state. Other companies are building in stress management approaches, but these are more often in the form of a lecture than an ongoing approach. I look forward to the day when people work for a while, then exercise, then work, and then meditate or work in the garden adjoining the plant. I look forward to the day when eating meals at work becomes an exercise in consciousness shifting rather than throwing some junk down the machine to keep it running. We are not machines, yet we often treat ourselves like machines. The problem is, we can't just drain our oil and start clean like machines.

AWAKENING OUR CONSCIOUSNESS TO THE ENVIRONMENT

One important shift in consciousness involves integrating more humane treatment of our environment, believing that this will produce more prosperity in the long run. When the predominant value is making money at all costs, when companies build in the number of cancer deaths as an economic cost, when our forests are devastated and the greenhouse effect and other disastrous environmental effects increase, then we are out of balance. There is no real democracy because we are listening primarily to one voice—the voice of greed. What about the voice of balance, the voice valuing health more than wealth, the voice that values environmental beauty more than quick profits? Listening to these voices produces a shift in what we value, and therefore how we live.

One of the fundamental shifts that occurs as we move more into a psychological democracy is that our male and female parts come more into balance and integration. The hatred, distrust, and repression of women, in particular, by men, will come to an end as we begin to embrace the feminine side of ourselves. This means for men that we can't split off our emotional sides. We need to move forward, but we also need to feel what we are doing. I have seen the costs to the Earth of not doing this. I also know from my experience working with corporate executives that those who turn their feeling selves off in order to exploit people and the environment suffer because they treat themselves, their partners, and their families in the same way. Whenever we oppress others, we oppress ourselves.

I have worked with women who can't access certain kinds of inner powers they need to move forward in life because they associate these qualities with being male. These gender issues need to be processed through individual, couple, family, large group, and worldwork formats. The more we work to pick up qualities that we associate as "other," the more whole we become, and the more fulfilling our relationships are, no matter what their form. The more of ourselves we bring to relationship, the more fulfillment is possible.

This shift will have tremendous political repercussions. We have seen incredible changes in the workplace as the oppression of women lifts and changes. Another major place these changes will manifest is the increasing development of a worldwide ecology movement. As people open to their own feminine energy, they also open to the archetypal energy of the Mother Earth. As we have treated the feminine side of ourselves, and women in general, so have we treated the Earth, universal symbol of feminine energy. As this shift in consciousness occurs, people will simply not be able to do to the Earth what they have done in the past.

Also, the whole idea of exploiting workers needs to shift, so that we understand, as more and more companies do, that the well-being of employees and the well-being of companies are linked. In the old way, work is seen as owners and management versus workers. In the new way, owners will see that workers' well-being is intimately connected to the well-being of the owner and the company, and workers will grow in their understanding that they also have owners inside of them, and understand more where the owners are coming from. Owners will grow in their understanding that workers everywhere, no matter what color, country, class, or education level, want some of the same things for their lives and families that the owners do. We need to make progress so that corporation heads don't make millions per year, while so many workers in many countries make pennies per hour. As consciousness shifts to the realization of the connectedness of all beings, it is possible that inequities will begin to shift. Already there has been pressure, for example, on tennis shoe manufacturers to change how they treat workers in Third World countries.

While we have made some small progress in treating the Earth differently, the battle for domination goes on, particularly in areas where the predominant culture wants the uranium and other natural materials that the earth can yield. Many of these natural materials are on Native soil. The government is attempting to take back the Native land, which it did not want until precious metals, coal, and oil were discovered under those lands. Much of the repression of Native culture has to do with needing to repress taking care of the earth, since caring for the earth is bad for short-term business gains. There is a Native American expression that says people need to think seven generations down the line before they act in regard to the Earth. Maybe we will never return to this state of awareness, but even if we think two generations down, to our own great-grandchildren, or if we think of what is going to happen in our own lifetime, beyond this quarter's profits, we will have to change. Aboriginal people in Australia, tribal people in the Amazon, and people from many other places in the world remind us of the sacredness of the Earth.

Much of what we do comes from simple lack of awareness. When I was involved in a movement to stop spraying herbicides, I heard people in favor of herbicides tell stories of letting their animals drink herbicides containing dioxin, one of the world's most toxic chemicals. These people were not malicious; they were simply not aware of the short- and long-term effects of toxic chemicals and were happy to allow themselves, their families, and their friends to be sprayed.

As our consciousness changes, we begin to dream that our physical bodies are sacred, as is the Earth. A woman I once bought goats from told me the following story: Her life had been tough, and her mother difficult. One day she had to let out some of her personal pain, even though she was shy, so she went into her garden and began to scream and cry. She suddenly found herself curled up on the ground in a fetal position and had an experience of the earth becoming her mother and healing her. She said for the first time in a long time she felt at peace. This was not a New Age explorer pushing the outer limits of consciousness, but an ordinary country person, certainly more open to herself and experiences and telling about them than most people.

More and more people are experiencing the healing power of nature. I once dreamed that the sky was my father. We are awakening to a new-old consciousness, and our changes in consciousness have significant environmental effects. As changes keep occurring in men's consciousness, we become strong based on our wholeness, including our vulnerability. We own our strength and reject being sexist and repressing women and ourselves.

I remember one incredibly courageous woman who came from generations of loggers and was married to a logger. At one point, she had a shift in consciousness and realized that trees have consciousness. She began to talk to her husband and his logger friends about this. What courage this took. People listened to her because of the family she came from. If I had talked to loggers about the importance of how you treat the trees, I would have been considered insane. She was on the inside, though. She persisted, telling the men that they needed to talk to the trees before they cut them, honor them, and try to cut with consciousness. Believe it or not, eventually, this started to work. Some of the men, including her husband, began to try to communicate with the trees before they were cut. They said their work has taken on a different feeling since then. They have also become more sensitive to issues like clear-cutting and cutting old growth, balancing their ecological needs and their economic needs to feed their families. They are even more proud to be loggers. Many men carry this sensitivity and love for nature when we hike, raft, fish, and hunt. It hurts us to have to shut it off when we are asked to at work.

There are real concerns about shifts in consciousness. Jobs are important, and any environmental group that promotes trees without thinking about people is one-sided. The people who work in the forest and in forest products industries are our friends and neighbors. As someone who cares about trees, I also don't want to hurt these people. However, I am confident that we can find environmentally and economically sound solutions. Some proposals show that working in a more ecological way will mean more long-term economic health for the forest industry.

Organic gardening is similar. Several major studies comparing yields from organic and non-organic methods showed that there is not much difference in yield and a tremendous difference in economic savings. Organic farming feeds the soil and doesn't poison the farmer or threaten the consumer. The long-term studies show that organic farming makes economic sense. Several farms, including Lundberg rice farms in California, are well known for their transition to organic methods. The recent scare over alar in apples caused such uproar that major companies such as Safeway began stocking organic foods. We have come a long way from the ridicule that met the first organic farmers.

The *Tao Te Ching*, an ancient Chinese book of wisdom, says that anything in harmony with nature will last, while what is out of harmony will perish. When I make business decisions, I try to keep this in mind. If I push myself as hard as I can to make as much money as I can as fast as I can, I may lose my enjoyment of life. I believe working in sustainable ways is the only way that will work, and individuals, businesses, and governments who don't move toward sustainability will disappear. I want to be successful in business, and I believe that being in harmony with nature brings me the best chance of success. We need to think of ourselves as human resources.

All over the world, people are involved in major battles to stop the land from being further polluted. I moved to the Northwest partially because of my love of nature. Now when I go riding near my house, I notice the latest clear-cut, then the not-so-recent clear cuts, and yet there is still beautiful forest left.

What will we do when there are no more places of beauty and power where people can go to recharge their spirits? I once heard a federal official say that he didn't believe there was such a thing as an endangered species. I also remember a Native American leader who said that when all the wild animals are killed, humans would die of the loneliness in their souls. We are not far from that point.

It is clear that the growing wave of more democratic, ecologically based living has to be developed for us to survive. Small towns are an ideal spot to develop this new consciousness. The independent spirit, connection with nature, and growing crises in rural economic systems make these places fertile ground for such changes. Changes happen most organically from the inside out. As people develop psychologically with the help of counseling, changes can take root and spread throughout the land.

When she was four, my daughter and I were talking about our area's decision to resume roadside herbicide spraying. She said to me "Daddy, why are they doing that? The earth is special." Not only is the earth special, but the earth and spirit we are made up of as human beings are special.

How many people do you know who value and have access to all the parts of themselves? Do you know anyone who lives in a true internal democracy? Most of us haven't reached true inner democracy, but many of us are growing in this direction. Groups may not be able to grow faster than the individuals in a group. Our greatest hopes and dreams for true world peace and democracy may emerge out of the tremendous interest in personal growth spreading throughout the world. If we can respect all the parts of ourselves, we are on the road to a global democracy. As we create internal democracy, then work on similar problems in our world, we move from victims of our modern world to enlightened co-creators of a new world, a world that we can look forward to living in, and welcoming the next generations into.

My experiences working with small towns make me both a realist and an optimist. Realistically, I know how difficult some of the problems we face are. Nevertheless, I am optimistic because I have seen, and deeply believe in, the power of grassroots change. We only have to look at some of the changes in eastern Europe in recent years, as people chose to move out of communism, to know the power of the people.

Change needs to be wedded to consciousness. Social change is intrinsically connected with individual, relationship, and small and large group work. The simplest way to change is to begin with what's closest at hand and then move outward. We can learn at the local level and then move to issues that affect more and more people. Begin with yourself. As you become freer inside, you are in a better position to help your family, friends, neighborhood, town, city, state, country, and world.

THERAPISTS AND WORLD CHANGE

Therapists are in a special position to facilitate change, beginning at the small town level and working outward. I'd like to make a special appeal to therapists—go to the small towns near you and start seeing people, even if you open a little office and see people one day each week. Counseling and psychology have become so popular that I know many new therapists who can't find work, or want to do a private practice but end up at an agency. Consider small towns. Many times there are towns close to wherever you live, so you can commute. Commuting down a country highway is more pleasant than fighting traffic to go downtown. You may not only end up helping a lot of people who need help, but also build yourself a great practice. You may find yourself doing work you have always wanted to do in a setting you never dreamed of doing it in.

As therapists, we need to wake up to the social and political implications of our therapeutic interventions. We need to be more than behavior changers who help people adjust to an increasingly disturbed world; we need to realize that part of helping people grow is helping sensitize them to what is happening around them. We can help empower people to make a difference in changing the world.

We need to risk leaving our offices and taking our skills into local, national, and global situations that require skilled facilitation. Often, when we think of saving endangered species, we think of whales or eagles. Saving these animals, and many others, is crucial. However, we often forget that people are an endangered species. In huge areas of this country when people need help, people have no access to counseling; this is terribly destructive, since much inner pain and outer violence is preventable. Assisting in a shift in consciousness is a task of nearly impossible magnitude, and reaching the bulk of the people in this country, even if we could open a counseling agency in every small town in America, is impossible. However, reaching everyone may not be necessary. Physicist Rupert Sheldrake has postulated that if a certain portion of the field changes, if a critical mass is reached, if enough members of a field make a change, the whole field will change. We may be able to shift our world by changing others, one by one, and ourselves.

The field of counseling needs to help this shift in consciousness by moving beyond our narrow focus. Private practice continues to focus primarily on middle-class, white, educated people in cities and suburbs. If we are going to turn the corner to be a more conscious society, this narrow focus has to change. Health insurance has provided a great service to people by paying licensed professionals for outpatient mental health care. Many more people can afford counseling by utilizing their health insurance benefits. One of the complaints many therapists have is that their work becomes boring because they hear the same things over and over. Working as a therapist in a small town is a sure way to add some variety, and many people in small towns would love help, but there are no therapists available.

We need to utilize our whole selves, including our personal development and our concern for social issues, and become facilitators of change in the world.

The world needs not only highly skilled and evolved therapists, but therapists who are world workers and can facilitate world change.

CHANGING THE WORLD

As we grow and develop, our changes spread outward to the people we touch. The more we change, the more the field changes. Every little bit helps.

Am I a dreamer, hoping for an impossible change in consciousness? Maybe I am, but who would have dreamt that the civil rights movement would make such huge progress? Who would have dreamt that the structure of eastern Europe would change so dramatically, so rapidly? To truly change, we must respect our own beings enough to help them develop and to let ourselves be who we are. Changing our inner attitudes is the first step in changing the outer world. I remember a line from John Lennon's song "Imagine": "You may say I am the dreamer, but I am not the only one. I hope someday you will join us, so the world can live as one." Lennon is dead, but his plea lives on.

Without the foundation of internal change, we can pass legislation and make rules to protect the environment, but the spirit won't be right for change. A leap in consciousness needs a backbone to build on. Just as small towns were the backbone of rapid industrial and economic growth, they could also be the backbone for the leap in consciousness that integrates economic growth with a spiritual and psychological awareness. This would be a leap towards a true ecology of being that permeates all aspects of our life.

In a system based on ecology of being, we will need to shift from materialistic values to values that emphasize the quality of being. We need a standard of living that measures not only the televisions per capita, but how satisfying and meaningful people find life. In a society full of psychological and spiritual suffering, we have a long way to go. Material happiness is certainly a step in the right direction. If one follows Maslow's idea that people have a hierarchy of needs, with survival at the bottom of the ladder and self-actualization at the top, we need the bottom rungs, but also the top. Societies can stagnate at the level of material well-being, and ignore the other rungs that survival is a stepping stone to. In a society based on ecology of being, all parts of human existence are valued and supported. When we value all of each other, and ourselves, we value all of nature, and in harmony we can reach the heights of meaningful existence.

Another crucial piece of well-being is to share our material wealth with others. Achieving material happiness is a privilege that most of the world does not have. The top hundred billionaires in the world have more combined wealth than the two and a half billion people who have the least. Having people with so much they could never spend it all, while a large part of the world goes hungry, is not sustainable.

The choice is up to all of us, and turning the course of history will require many of us taking responsibility for the next steps. The dream of true democracy is possible within our life times, as is the choice of environmental destruction or nuclear annihilation. We need to co-create a lifestyle that helps people develop and encourages their moving towards living as enlightened human beings, together as one planet.

SUGGESTED REFERENCES

Beattie, Melody. *Co-Dependent No More*. Center City, MN: Hazelden, 1989.

Bobo, Kim and Kendell, Jackie. *Organizing for Social Change*. Washington: Seven Locks Press, 1991.

Buber, Martin. *I and Thou,* New York: Scribner, 1970.

Diamond, Jed. *The Warrior's Journey Home*. Oakland, CA: New Harbringer, 1994.

Dworkin, Jan. "Group Process Work: A Stage for Personal and Global Development." Unpublished dissertation, Union Institute, Cincinnati, OH, 1989.

Chinen, Allan. *Beyond the Hero*. New York: Putnam, 1993.

Chinen, Allan. *In the Ever After: Fairy Tales and the Second Half of Life*. Wilmette, IL: Chiron, 1990.

Feng, Gia-Fu. *Tao Te Ching*. New York: Vintage Books/ Random House, 1972.

Garfield, Patricia. *Creative Dreaming*. New York: Simon & Schuster, 1995.

Hanh, Thich Naht. *Being Peace*. Berkeley, CA: Parallax Press, 1988.

Hillman, James. *Dream Animals*, San Francisco, CA: Chronicle Books, 1997.

Hillman, James and Ventura, Michael. *We've Had a Hundred Years of Psychotherapy and the World's Getting Worse*. San Francisco: Harper, 1993.

Keyes, Ken. *The Hundredth Monkey*. Coos Bay, OR: Vision Books, 1982.

Leonard, Linda. *Witness to the Fire: Creativity and the Veil of Addiction.* Boston & Shaftesbury: Shambhala, 1989.

Mathews, Forrest David, *Politics for People*: Urbana: University of Illinois Press, 1994.

Mindell, Amy, *Metaskills The Spiritual Art of Therapy.* Tempe, AZ: New Falcon, 1995.

Mindell, Amy and Mindell, Arnold. *Riding the Horse Backwards.* London and New York: Viking-Penguin, 1992.

Mindell, Arnold. *Dreambody, The Body's Role in Revealing the Self.* Boston: Sigo Press, 1982. London and New York: Viking-Penguin-Arkana, 1985. Portland, OR: Lao Tse Press, 1998.

Mindell, Arnold. *River's Way.* New York and London: Viking-Penguin-Arkana, 1985.

Mindell, Arnold. *Working with the Dreaming Body.* New York and London: Viking-Penguin-Arkana, 1986.

Mindell, Arnold. *The Dreambody in Relationships.* New York and London: Viking-Penguin-Arkana, 1987.

Mindell, Arnold. *City Shadows: Psychological Interventions in Psychiatry.* New York and London: Viking-Penguin-Arkana, 1988.

Mindell, Arnold. *Coma: The Dreambody Near Death.* New York and London: Arkana, 1994

Mindell, Arnold. *Working on Yourself Alone.* New York and London: Viking-Penguin-Arkana, 1989.

Mindell, Arnold. *The Year I: Global Process Work with Planetary Myths and Structures.* New York and London: Viking-Penguin-Arkana, 1989.

Mindell, Arnold. *Sitting in the Fire.* Portland, OR: Lao Tse Press, 1995.

Moore, Robert and Douglas Gillette. *King, Warrior, Magician, Lover.* San Francisco: Harper San Francisco, 1990.

Pulster, Irving. *Gestalt Therapy Integrated.* New York: Vintage Books, 1974.

Ross, Marilyn and Ross, Tom. *Country Bound.* Buena Vista, CO: Communication Creativity, 1992.

Rotherenberg, Michael. Wildfire Magazine, Vol. 4, No. 1, Bear Tribe Publishing.

Sheldrake, Rupert. *A New Science of Life: The Hypothesis of Formative Causation.* Los Angeles: Tarcher, 1981.

Sun Bear, and Wabun, and Niminosha. *The Bear Tribe's Self-Reliance Book.* New York: Prentice Hall Press, 1988.

Suzuki, David and Knudtson, Peter. *Wisdom of the Elders: Sacred Native Stories of Nature.* New York: Bantam Books, 1993.

Weil, Andrew. *Natural Health, Natural Medicine: A Comprehensive Manual for Wellness and Self-Care.* Boston: Houghton Mifflin, 1990.

Weiss, Elizabeth. *The Anger Trap*, New York: Philosophical Library, 1984.

West, Cornell. *Race Matters.* New York: Vintage Books, 1993.

About the Author

Gary Reiss, LCSW, is a licensed clinical social worker and has his diploma in process-oriented psychology. He has been in private practice for twenty-seven years. Gary teaches process-oriented psychology worldwide. He is on the faculty of the Process Work Center of Portland. He has offices in Eugene, Cottage Grove and Portland, Oregon, and is director of a counseling clinic in rural Oregon.

One of Gary's special interest in process work includes conflict work. He works extensively in Israel, India, Australia and other hot spots in the world. He also has special interests integrating process work with other spiritual traditions and working with people in, and coming out of, comatose states.

He has a strong interest in several spiritual traditions including mystical Judaism, shamanism, and Native American approaches. He integrates his psychological work with these different traditions.

His work has been published in several newspapers and journals. He is currently working on three other books: *Transforming Family Life: Process Oriented Couple, Family and Sex Therapy*; *Angry Men, Angry World: A Process Oriented Psychology Approach to Anger*; and *Becoming Eagle: Moving from Fear of Life and Death to Flying Freely*.

He regularly appears on radio shows to talk about working on issues of racism, diversity and many other topics.

Gary lives in the country and enjoys spending time with his family, his garden, and his horses. He is an avid skier and runner and loves learning about all the intricacies of life.